*O*CCUPY TILL I COME

GALADIMA BITRUS

i

OCCUPY TILL I COME

By

Galadima Bitrus

All Enquiries To
+234 (0)903 405 3324

Designed, @DgalaGraphiz
Email: dgala0019@gmail.com
+234 (0)8147163578 +234 (0)7052404294

Table of Contents

DEDICATION

This book is dedicated to my wife (Gift B. G.) who was kidnapped and my elder brother Joshua B. G. who was killed by bandits during the invasion of 14th of April, 2023.

ACKNOWLEDGMENTS

A grand work such as this cannot be completely done by just one man. So many persons worked closely with me to bring this book to fruition.

Gift B. G. (my wife) did the listening while this book was audibly read at it its initial stage to ensure it will make sense to the listener, her contributions were great and helped to shape this book into what it is now.

Reverend Jonathan Madaki (Secretary, ECWA Kaffi DCC) was always in my house to ascertain the progress of this work and kept me on my toes to ensure its fast completion. His editorial suggestions opened my horizon to the concept of multiple streams of income discussed in this book.

Dauda B. G. did the typesetting and I delegated Stephen A. A.'s to take up some of my responsibilities to enable me focus on this book and to ensure it reaches your hands! Zumunci Y. B. and Pastor Amos Tukura are fathers whose encouragement stirs me to soar high.

Finally to my son Ọnọmtọna Augustine Bitrus (Galadima Jr.) I appreciate those times you had endure my absence.

SECTION A

INTRODUCTION

1

Coming With The Clouds

Last year 2022, the Evangelical Church Winning All (ECWA) adopted a theme "Behold, he is coming with the clouds." This was fetched from Revelation 1:7

> *"Behold, he is coming with the clouds, and every eye will see him, everyone who pierced him; and all tribes of the earth will wail on account of him. Even so. Amen."* **RSV**

My church pastor introduced the theme and told us that sermons in ECWA that year were going to dig more into the end times with much to be drawn from the book of Daniel and Revelation.

And to the glory of God, ECWA members worldwide were blessed with messages that surround very controversial topics that many clergies mostly avoid. Such topics include "The Rapture," "The Great Tribulation," "The Judgement," "The Antichrist," "The Four Beasts of the book of Daniel," "The Dragon and the Woman," "The Great Tribulation Versus The Rapture," etc.

The book of Revelation is often treated with fear and carefulness for fear of the verses that says:

> *"I give fair warning to all who hear the words of the prophecy of this book: If you add to the words of this prophecy, God will add to your life the disasters written in this book; if you subtract from the words of the book of this prophecy, God will subtract your part from the Tree of Life and the Holy City that are written in this book."*
> **Revelation *22:18-19* MSG**

Many Christian preachers including me are very careful in dealing with this book because of the implication contained in it. All books in the Bible are God's breath but the books are not all the same in their gravity.

All the books are important and must never be misinterpreted but the consequences of misinterpreting the books vary from one book to another. Base on the verses above, an addition of anything to it or subtraction of anything from the book of Revelation is very dangerous. God will punish everyone who misinterpret any verse of the Bible but that of the last book of the Bible will be more severe.

The warning is against any alteration in the contents of the book, either adding material to it or deleting (omitting) something from it. Such additions or deletions would change the message and would therefore bring punishment from God.

It is this fear that binds many preachers from attempting to preach from it. However, this ought not to be so. That verse is not a restraining order to Christian preachers and teachers but rather a motivation for an in-depth study of the book before preaching it.

If I were to paraphrase part of that verse, I will say something like this: *"Be careful to ensure that you do not translate or interpret this book to say what it did not say and also be careful and do not fail to say what this book says."*

Whatever be the case, the year have actually come and gone. And a new theme is adopted for this year, 2023. But I love to say a few things about last year's theme before I deal fully with the present theme.

I Preached Last Year

Last year, I was invited a couple of times to preach on the theme *"Behold, he is coming with the clouds."* On two occasions I was invited to talk to a group of singles (the unmarried) on this topic "Singles Waiting for the coming of Christ."

To the glory of God, the service was edifying. Let me pick on a few things from the talk:

A. Single persons are defined in our society as those who are unmarried. A single person is one who is not yoked to anyone at the present in the name of marriage.

They have less concerns and troubles. Their thoughts are not yet chocked with troubles of marriage, children, in-laws, etc.

Such persons fall into three categories:
- ❖ Those who have never married.
- ❖ Those who married but are presently unmarried (divorced).
- ❖ Those who married but their partner is late (widow/widower).

Marriage and singleness are not permanent states. A single person can marry today and seize to be a single person.

However, his/her partner can die today or tomorrow and the person is back to his single state. Divorce also can bring two married people back into singleness.

Just a thin line separates marriage from singleness. The door out of singleness is just one – marriage, but there are three doors into singleness:

i. Birth: Everyone is born unmarried, which is singleness. From the womb everyone is recruited into singleness.

ii. Death: A married person who is not single is immediately ushered into singleness the moment death visits his/her partner.

iii.   Divorce: This is another door through which many persons are escaping into singleness. They escaped singleness into marriage and when it becomes tough, they or their partner goes for a divorce. There and then, the two make a sojourn back into singleness.

B.   As singles, persons with much less troubles of life, you must engage yourselves in productive labors. Yes, Jesus is coming with the clouds but you must not sit and fold your arms while waiting for him.

In the days of Paul many believers thought that the eminent return of Christ was going to be in their days. So, they thought if Christ was coming immediately to take believers back home, why should they strive to establish anything on earth.

Some even became literally idle; they said if you plant a vineyard, Jesus will return before you start reaping the fruit of your labor. This wrong perception still prevails among some believers today.

I have a neighbor called Sunday Jacob Shalom. He planted an orchard of about one thousand oil palm trees. His friend Pastor Zamani Amale also did same. As of 2022, the plantations were already producing and both of them were already reaping from their labors.

I was discussing with him one faithful afternoon and he told me this:

"Galadima, you know Pastor Zamani and Pastor Nebuchadnezzar are my close friends. The idea of raising a plantation was sold to us together but Pastor Nebuchadnezzar refused to accept it because he felt before the plantation matures and bring forth fruits, Jesus would have return. However, after about 10 years now, Jesus is not yet back and we are already enjoying the fruit of our labors. Currently, Pastor Nebuchadnezzar is regretting his decision and wish he had joined us to also raise a plantation then."

Today, Sunday Jacob Shalom is late but the plantation continues to live and his family is benefiting from it.

The problem here is a matter of the timing of his coming. If Christ says "I am coming with the clouds," it then becomes necessary to try to understand how long it may take before his return. It is important for believers to study the *"When"* of his coming.

If Christ were to return tomorrow, then I would have stopped writing this book today because before it gets to your hands or the hands of anyone, Jesus is here already. If Christ were to come next year, I shall not suffer myself to establish any fruit plantation because it will be a fruitless labor.

Many brethren touched into error over the "*When*" of his coming. Trying to study available clues that points to the timing of Christ's second coming is not a forbidden adventure because such clues abounds in the holy word of God.

However, there have been a number of "brethren" who at some points in time predicted the exact date that Christ will return. This is an error because Jesus declared that such knowledge is exclusively reserved for and by the Father alone. Not even the angels of God in heaven know of such a date and so it is absolutely unbiblical to try to predict that.

I so believed that it is important that we understand the timing of this command so that some of us will not refuse to make long term plans for the future.

"*Behold He is coming with the clouds*" describes the return of the glorified Christ to the world, and the clouds are, so to speak, his means of transportation (Psalms 104.3b). The present tense "*he comes*" describes the event as taking place in the immediate future; but interpreters must never say he is coming now, at the time of this event.

The theme really portrays how quick Christ will return but does not mean he is coming now. This is where I very much appreciate the current theme of ECWA: "*Trade with This Money until I Return*," which is popularly rendered as "*Occupy Till I Come.*"

This theme tells us that yes Christ is coming but not today and that while we wait for his coming, we must not be idle. There is a task he left for each believer to do before he returns.

Between now and when the master will return, there are responsibilities we must discharge. There are certain duties he left for us to carry out. We are not just going to be idling around neither are we expected to be busybodies while he is away. We are to "Occupy till he comes" (*Trade with This Money until He Return*)

2

Occupy Till I Come

The ECWA theme of the year 2023 is "Occupy Till I Come". This is rendered in Ẹda language as "*Unu du itrim lẹ ikli lẹn se imi eywure*" which when literally translated means "You (*plural*) should trade with this money till I return."

'*Ku yi kasuwanci da su sai na dawo.*' **HCL**

'*Trade with these till I come.*' **RSV**

'*Operate with this until I return.*' **MSG**

"*Use this money to get more money for me while I am away,*" **EASY TO READ**

'*Invest this for me while I am gone.*' **NLT**

'*Put this money to work,*' he said, '*until I come back.*' **NIV**

'*Put this money to work until I come back*' **NIRV**

'*Make use of it till I come.*' **TMBA**

"Conduct business until I come." **OJB**

'See what you can earn with this while I am gone.' **GNTA**

'Engage in business until I come back.' **CSB**

Virtually all translations agree that the word translated to mean *"Occupy"* does not really and clearly convey the instruction of the master. The word *"Occupy"* as a transitive verb gives the following meanings:

- ✓ To live in or be the established user of a place such as a home or office

- ✓ To take up somebody's time or attention (often passive)

- ✓ To fill up a space. It is to take up a space or an amount of time (often passive)

- ✓ The military take-over of a place: to invade and take control of a country, area, or building

- ✓ It means to hold a position or rank

The word came to use in the 14th century. Via Old French *occuper* < Latin *occupare* "take over" < *capere* "to take"[1]

---

[1] Microsoft® Encarta® 2009. © 1993-2008 Microsoft Corporation.

If this be the only understanding of the word "Occupy", then the theme can be paraphrased as:

"Take control of this home/country till I return."
"Take control of this money until I return."

There will actually be no problem with this interpretation because it will mean Christ is urging us to occupy as much hearts as possible for him. He wants us to take charge of our nations for him while he is away and before he returns.

But we have two problems with that perception

1. When the master came, he did not ask them what and what position or space they occupied. He simply requires an account of what each of them did with the *minas* he gave them.

2. The Greek word that is translated to mean "*Occupy*" is Πραγματεύσασθε (*pragmateusasthe*). This word speaks of Trade and investment.

A literal word for word (Greek to English) exegesis of the text (Luke 19:13) gives the following:

kalesas de deka doulous heautou lit. 'after calling ten slaves of his', i.e. 'ten of his slaves'.

edōken autois deka mnas 'he gave them ten *minas*', i.e. one each. (*mna* 'mina', is a Greek monetary unit of about eighteen to twenty dollars.)

pragmateusasthe en hō erchomai 'do business until I come back'.

That is, a true literal exegesis of the text is "He summoned his ten servants and gave them ten *minas* each and told them to trade with/do business with/invest the *minas* until he returns.

Therefore, a more transparent translation of the verse is the one found in Ẹda language, Ẹhua, Jijili and Ajigha languages. RSV, NLT, HCL, GNTA and NIV amongst others are also on the list of translations that translated the verse clearly from the source language (Greek) to their recipient languages.

Please note that I am not doing this exegesis to condemn or discredit the NKJV translation. I did this to settle the seeming confusion that many indigenous languages seems to have in blending their own indigenous translation with the NKJV.

Introduction of the book of Luke
The theme is fetched from the book of Luke chapter 19 verses 13. So, it necessary to understand a few things about the book; the book of Luke is a carefully investigated and an orderly compiled narrative of the things which have been accomplished. It was written by Doctor Luke (who was a physician and a believer of our Lord Jesus Christ.)

Luke was probably not Jewish. He wrote this book some time between the years AD 59 and AD 80. For some reasons, some people think that he wrote this book in the city called Rome. He wrote it for an important friend called Theophilus who most likely was a Roman official.

Luke also intends the book for other disciples of Jesus so that they would know Jesus better. Then they could answer questions when people asked them about him. Many people had wrong ideas about Jesus and Luke wanted people to know what was true.

Luke tells us the good news about the kingdom of God. That means that God wants to rule in the lives of his people. Those people may be Jewish or they may be Gentiles (not Jewish). Luke tells us about Jesus' birth. He also tells us about his life and his death.

He explains to us why Jesus came to the world and what he did during his life here. Then he tells us how he went back to heaven to live with his Father God again. At the end, Luke explains to us about God's gift of his Holy Spirit.

Jesus had told people a message that was good news. Now Jesus wanted his disciples to tell that message to everyone in the world. Luke wanted everyone to know what Jesus said and what he did so he wrote this book.

The Gospel of Luke is basically in four parts:

> **1.** What happened before Jesus started his work (1:1—4:13).

2. What happened when Jesus was working in Galilee (4:14—9:50).
3. What happened when Jesus was working in Judea and Perea (9:51—19:27).
4. What happened in Jerusalem in the last week of Jesus' life (19:28—24:53).

From the outline above, Galilee, Judea and Perea were regions of the country that is called Israel while Jerusalem was the capital city of Israel at that time.

However, a broader outline is presented as this:

A. Introduction (1.1-4)
B. Birth and Childhood of John the Baptist and of Jesus (1.5–2.52). The Birth of John the Baptist is Announced (1.5-25)
    1. The Birth of Jesus is Announced (1.26-38)
    2. Mary Visits Elizabeth (1.39-45)
    3. Mary's Song of Praise (1.46-56)
    4. The Birth of John the Baptist (1.57-66)
    5. Zechariah's Prophecy (1.67-80)
    6. The Birth of Jesus (2.1-7)
    7. The Shepherds and the Angels (2.8-20)
    8. Jesus Is Named (2.21)
    9. Jesus is Presented in the Temple (2.22-39)
    10. The Return to Nazareth (2.39-40)
    11. The Boy Jesus in the Temple (2.41-52)
C. Preparation for Jesus' ministry (3.1–4.13)
    1. Ministry of John the Baptist (3.1-20)

      a. Jesus Prays on the Mount of Olives (22.39-46)

      b. The Arrest of Jesus (22.47-53)

      c. Peter Denies Jesus (22.54-62)

      d. Jesus Is Mocked and Beaten (22.63-65)

      e. Jesus before the Council (22.66-71)

      f. Jesus before Pilate (23.1-5)

      g. Jesus before Herod (23.6-12)

      h. Jesus Is Sentenced to Death (23.13-25)

      i. Jesus Is Crucified (23.26-43)

      j. The Death of Jesus (23.44-49)

      k. The Burial of Jesus (23.50-56)

  3. Resurrection and ascension of Jesus (24.1-53)

      a. The Resurrection (24.1-12)

      b. The Walk to Emmaus (24.13-35)

      c. Jesus Appears to His Disciples (24.36-49)

      d. Jesus Is Taken Up to Heaven (24.50-53)

Luke was not an eye witness of the things he was reporting to Theophilus in this book but some people were present when all these things started and happened and Luke gathered his report from them.

Luke's information was second hand. However, he checked, studied and gathered the facts about what really happened in the earthly days of Jesus Christ before writing to make the facts clear to his disciple Theophilus.

The books: Luke and Acts of the Apostles are two volumes of a single work. Together they tell the story of how God first invited the people of Israel, and then all nations, to follow Jesus.

In the first volume, the movement is toward Jerusalem, the center of Jewish national life. In the second, the movement is from Jerusalem to other nations, closing with Paul proclaiming the kingdom of God in Rome, the capital of the empire.

The two volumes are stocked with details from sources that Luke had available: letters, speeches, songs, travel accounts, trial transcripts and biographical anecdotes.

Luke was a medical doctor and a believer of the Lord Jesus Christ. How he became a believer is not stated in scriptures but it is mentioned in scriptures that he was among the disciples that stayed close to Paul.

Paul associated closely with young and upcoming Christian leaders. He kept them around him and groomed them. His association with Luke developed and advanced Luke's leadership potential and turned the Physician into an author of great books "Acts of the Apostle and the Gospel of Luke."

Paul's life was open to young people to learn from and that freedom and unhindered access into all he knew turned new born babes in the faith to mighty men of God.

From the Gospel of Luke, 13 parables are found and the parable of the ten *minas* is one of them.

SECTION B

PARABLE OF THE TEN MINAS

3

The Parable of the Ten *Minas*

¹¹*While they were listening to this, he went on to tell them a parable, because he was near Jerusalem and the people thought that the kingdom of God was going to appear at once.* ¹²*He said: "A man of noble birth went to a distant country to have himself appointed king and then to return.*

¹³*So he called ten of his servants and gave them ten minas. 'Put this money to work,' he said, 'until I come back.'* ¹⁴*"But his subjects hated him and sent a delegation after him to say, 'We don't want this man to be our king.'*

¹⁵*"He was made king, however, and returned home. Then he sent for the servants to whom he had given the money, in order to find out what they had gained with it.* ¹⁶*"The first one came and said, 'Sir, your mina has earned ten more.'*

¹⁷" 'Well done, my good servant!' his master replied. 'Because you have been trustworthy in a very small matter, take charge of ten cities.' ¹⁸"The second came and said, 'Sir, your mina has earned five more.'

¹⁹"His master answered, 'You take charge of five cities.' ²⁰"Then another servant came and said, 'Sir, here is your mina; I have kept it laid away in a piece of cloth. ²¹I was afraid of you, because you are a hard man. You take out what you did not put in and reap what you did not sow.'

²²"His master replied, 'I will judge you by your own words, you wicked servant! You knew, did you, that I am a hard man, taking out what I did not put in, and reaping what I did not sow? ²³Why then didn't you put my money on deposit, so that when I came back, I could have collected it with interest?'

²⁴"Then he said to those standing by, 'Take his mina away from him and give it to the one who has ten minas.' ²⁵" 'Sir,' they said, 'he already has ten!'

²⁶"He replied, 'I tell you that to everyone who has, more will be given, but as for the one who has nothing, even what they have will be taken away. ²⁷But those enemies

of mine who did not want me to be king over them—bring them here and kill them in front of me.'" **Luke 19:11-27**

Lesson 1: The Essence of the Parable of the *Minas*

"While they were listening to this, he went on to tell them a parable, because he was near Jerusalem and **the people thought that the kingdom of God was going to appear at once.***"*

Just like every other parable Jesus told his listeners, this parable was told for a reason; there was and is still an essence for this parable.

A parable is more of a story that conveys a meaning to the listener. Speaking and teaching in parables was Jesus' style of presenting core lessons of earthly and eternal life to people.

Speaking and teaching in parables engages the people as they rend their minds trying to find the true meaning of each parable told. At some points, the people are not able to personally unravel the true message contained in the parable and they have to ask Jesus. On other times, Jesus told the parables with their meaning while on other occasions, the people are able to decode the meaning of the parables.

Jesus often packaged spiritual truths and lessons of faith into short, relatable narratives known as parables. These stories were his way of explaining the attributes of God and instructions for godly living in accessible human terms.

And while Jesus also used sermons to communicate, his use of stories holds a special place in his ministry and teaching style.

Stories are memorable. They are relatable. They are easier to recall and share with others. For this reason, very few stories ever end with "the end."

A great story stays with you, and in the case of Jesus' parables, many of his listeners were still contemplating their application well beyond their initial telling, often arriving at the meaning of the message on their own, as opposed to simply being told.

The parable under consideration is tagged "*Parable of the Ten Minas,*" by some versions of the English language while some others puts it as "*Jesus tells a story about 10 servants,*" "*The Story About Investment,*" etc.

The present theme of ECWA is fetched from a parable that was told in order to correct a wrong notion that people were having concerning the appearance of the kingdom of God in the earth. The people were assuming 'that God's rule was to become visible in their days'. This parable was aimed at correcting their thoughts about the timing of Christ's kingdom.

Knowing or understanding the timing of God's kingdom is an underlying concern in the hearts of believers of all generations. The pressures of life are difficult and push us to be eager to know when our master is coming to rescue us from all these problems.

Again, we wish to figure out when Christ will return so that we will not engage ourselves in future plans that will not ripe before Jesus' return.

In the days of Jesus people held such beliefs and Jesus told them this parable. He told them this parable to help them understand that the kingdom of God was not to be revealed immediately. Yes, the kingdom of God would be revealed and established on the earth but this was not going to happen immediately.

The parable still speaks to us today and we learn from the very first verse of the parable that the kingdom of God will not be revealed immediately. But this must also never be misunderstood to mean that we have all the time to live here on earth. Jesus will come but we need to be occupied with some tasks he left for us before he returns.

And even if Jesus will not be revealed in our days, we must not forget that we are humans, we have a limited lifespan here on earth. Our stay here is temporal; the earth is a temporal abode. Even if Jesus did not return immediately, we will soon go the way of all mankind – death.

Lesson 2: **The Master Trust His Servants**

Jesus gave a story of a certain nobleman who went to a distant empire to be crowned king and then return. Before he left, he called together ten of his servants (*kalesas de deka doulous heautou*) and divided among them ten *minas* (*deka mnas*), saying, 'Invest this for me while I am gone.'

A *mna* 'mina', is a Greek monetary unit of about eighteen to twenty dollars. One mina was worth about three months' (one hundred days') wages of a laborer.

That is, the master gave each of the servants a huge treasure to trade with. Each servant received a treasure sufficient enough to pay for about one thousand (1000) days labor.

No one can give such a huge start-up capital to a group of people he never trusted. This therefore reveals that the master has confidence in the capacity of each of his servants. It proofs that the master is good enough to commit such a startup capital to his servants.

It is generally accepted among scholars and all Christian teachers that the master referred to here is Christ himself who went to heaven but left his servants behind to accomplish some tasks for him before his return. Jesus Christ did not leave his servants with no gifts when he ascended into heaven.

Like the master in the parable, Jesus Christ gave gifts to men when he ascended into the heavens. (Acts1, Ephesians 4).

Lesson 3: The Master Hates Idleness/Laziness

The master travelled alone leaving his servants behind just like Jesus ascended into the heavens alone. The master in the parable did not run to abandon his servants; neither did he abandon them to live idle lives just like Christ did not abandon his own followers to live idle lives.

Of a truth Jesus is the master discussed in this parable and this master hates laziness and idleness, so when he was travelling away, he left them with something to keep them busy and occupied.

Laziness

Psychology Today defines a lazy person as someone whose "motivation to spare himself effort trumps his motivation to do the right or expected thing." A lazy person is one who for the love of pleasure and ease, refuse to do what he can do which he ought to do.

He refuses to do what he ought to not necessarily because he is simply taking some time to rest but because he just wish to rest unnecessarily.

Laziness is a state of inactivity, inoperative state, been unoccupied, at rest, off, still, down, immobile. It speaks of indolence, shiftlessness, slothfulness (*formal*), sluggishness, and work-shyness.

A lazy person is one who loves sleep and enjoyment more than work. He can spend all his life playing video game and watching film but does not do any work. Such a person does not interfere with anyone's work but does not do his own work too.

Please mark the fact that a lazy person is a person who does not do his own work and will not interfere with another person's work. This is what distinguishes laziness from busybody.

I know that our culture today is a work-oriented society and so, taking a day or two off can be misunderstood for laziness. Our culture tethers us to our careers and a concept of productivity to the point where abstaining from those duties, even for a short while, evokes feelings of guilt and laziness.

And truly, we hate being labeled as lazy and so, relaxation is gradually becoming a thing of the past. Many persons are overworking themselves to death in an attempt to avoid been referred to as lazy people.

But if our view of laziness is of someone who takes one day off, then we must dismantle this perception of laziness in our society because taking breaks and catching our breaths is not laziness.

Consequences of Idleness/Laziness
- Idleness encourages dependence on other people.

• It retards the development of God given talents/abilities. Our gifts and our talents improve when we use them. If you are idle, your potentials will not be maximized. Idleness retards your potentials.

• It is seen as disobedience to Gods command for human beings to work.

• It may lead to antisocial and ungodly activities such as crime. Lack of trade is not why some people steal but it is one of the causes of stealing.

• It can lead to lifestyle diseases/it is unhealthy.

• It leads to poverty/lack of basic necessities. There are many Christians who are doing no business. They have no any source of income; they are living idle lives on the ground that "God will provide." You will find that such persons lack basic necessities of life: food, clothing, good medication, quality education, etc.

> *A little extra sleep, a little more slumber, a little folding of the hands to rest— then poverty will pounce on you like a bandit; scarcity will attack you like an armed robber.*   Proverbs 6:10-11

Today, Christians live very poor lives because they cannot afford the comfortable. Some Christians are plagued with a mindset that seems to portray serving God as a call to poverty. They think poverty is a virtue. But that is not so. Such a ideology is only true for those who takes the vow of poverty in the convent.

• Idleness may lead to conflicts/quarrels/fights among people. For example in marriages, if a wife is idle and depends completely on the man for every single need. Fight easily breaks out due to frustration. Such scenarios can be avoided if the woman finds a means of earning something no matter how small.

• It is failure to uphold the image of God as a worker.[2]

• Proverbs 10:4, 10:15, 11:24, 13:18, 14:23, 21:5, 22:16, 24:34, 28:22, 30:8, 31:7

Busybody

*[11] We hear that some among you are **idle** and disruptive. They are not busy; they are **busybodies**. [12] Such people we command and urge in the Lord Jesus Christ to **settle down and earn the food they eat.***

2 Thessalonians 3:11-12 NIV

*[13] Besides, they get into the habit of being **idle and going about from house to house**. And not only do they become **idlers**, but also **busybodies** who talk nonsense,*

---

2   https://www.atikaschool.org/cre-questions-and-answers/give-seven-reasons-why-christians-condemn-idleness-in-the-society

saying things they ought not to. ¹⁴So I counsel younger widows to marry, to have children, to manage their homes and to give the enemy no opportunity for slander.

1Timothy 5:13-14 NIV

Scriptures have something to say to us about being busybodies. Busybody is not a reference to a lifelong habit of laziness, but somehow the opposite. "Busybody" is different from "busy" and "Laziness/Idleness".

To be "**Busy**" means to be fully occupied in a particular activity, especially work. It is a state of not being free when one is committed to something that has previously been planned or arranged and so unable to undertake another activity. But **Laziness** is refusal to do what you ought to do which you can do and this is different from busybody.

The word **busybody** is completely different from the words "busy" and "laziness". From Greek, the word translated meddle (*busybody*) is περιεργαζομένους· (*periergazomenous·*). It means meddling in other people's business. It is to meddle in the affairs of someone else - to be a busybody.

It is similar to the word ἐργαζομένους (*ergazomenous*) which means to engage in an activity involving considerable expenditure of effort - to work, to labor, to be busy.

The two words περιεργαζομένους· (*periergazomenous·*) and ἐργαζομένους (*ergazomenous*) are the same. The only difference is the addition of the prefix περι (*peri*) which means "around", "run around uselessly".

This then gives us the meaning that a busybody is one who is busy running around other people's work. He is not only concerned with his own specific duty but puts his nose into other people's work.

He interferes with the work that is not his own. While his own work is not yet completed, he moves around to tell others how to do theirs. He moves around to do the work of others which he is not asked to do.

Such a person will be busy doing nothing; they cannot settle and focus their effort on a specific labor. They go about spreading false report and slandering others. Young widows are more susceptible to this.

But all categories of human beings are found in this class. The busybody virus does not know racial boundary, it is found among all races. Such people cause fights in the church and in Christian communities.

They are "idle in their own affairs, and interfering in everyone else's." They are such who live lazy lives and who do nothing except to meddle in other people's business.

They refuse to work in order to support themselves; however, they are constantly involved in other people's work," or "they are those who refuse to work for themselves but are busy meddling in other people's work."

The master did not want his servants to be idle and busybodies while he is gone and so, he gave each of them resources to engage in business while he is absent. If he had not given each one some mina, some people will have a reason to be idle while some will have justifiable reasons to go about meddling with the trades, businesses and investments of others.

In 2Corinthians 10:12-16, Paul the apostle explained that even apostles has their specific sphere or limit of operation. It simply means "an area over which a person has responsibility." Paul was given the specific appointment to preach to the gentiles.

In divvying up the responsibilities in the places where the apostles went, Paul had been given a certain sphere of influence, a sphere of responsibility, a sphere of authority; and he was not going to encroach into someone else's—Peter's or John's or any other's—area of responsibility.

So, Paul maintained that it would not be wise to move beyond what he had been given, and that he would not do that. He was going to go specifically to those people that God had told him to go to.

This is very important because in terms of the church, especially in terms of the ministry, apostles have been set apart for a specific responsibility. It is important for a minister not to go beyond that specific calling and appointment given to him.

But, we must not limit this appointment of responsibility just to apostles, just to ministers, or even to the church, or matters concerning the church, because God has given us all a sphere of influence, responsibility, and authority; and each one of those has limits.

And if any of us goes beyond his own sphere of influence, he/she is a busybody i.e. one who meddles in the affairs of others.

Let me conclude this section on busybody by saying Jesus gave us the best and most profound definition of a busybody when he said,

> *And why do you look at the speck in your brother's eye, but do not consider the plank in your own eye? Or how can you say to your brother, 'Let me remove the speck from your eye'; and look, a plank is in your own eye? Hypocrite! First remove the plank from your own eye, and then you will see clearly to remove the speck from your brother's eye.[3]*

---

[3] Matthew 7:3-5

From his statement, I deduce this solid definition of the term "Busybody." It is the neglect of your own big and enormous duties and responsibilities while running around seeking to attend to duties and responsibilities that are not yours.

The master does not want any of his servants to be lazy or busybody; he desired all of them to be duly engaged. That was why he gave each of them something to be busy with.

Lesson 4: **The *Minas* were not for fancy but for business**

The command the master gave his servant was *"pragmateusasthe en hō erchomai"* which is 'do business until I come back'. The Greek word *pragmateuomai* means 'to conduct business', or 'to trade'.

The words *en hō* 'during the time, which or while' as used here is equivalent to *heōs* 'until'. The master gave each of the servants some resources and charged them to do business with what he gave them until he returns.

It must be well noted that the master did not give them the money to go and use it to solve their personal problems. The money is not for them to buy cars, build houses and change new clothes. Again, we must pin it down that the *minas* each of them received was not a payment or a dismissal allowance.

It was given to them to do business with it. Meaning that whatever they had was not theirs but for the master. For, 'What do you have that have not been given to you?' Nothing! All that we have is that which we received. His gifts to us are not for fancy. His gifts are meant for business.

The concept of "Trade, Investment and Business" in the story tells us that the master is business minded. He does not accumulate treasures in water tanks and in his bedroom like some Nigerian leaders do.

He desires all his goods and resources to be put to productive and multiplicative use. The master is interested in business, multiplication and replication of resources.

And so, it is necessary for Christians to love business, trading, investments, merchandise, etc. No servant of the master must stay idle while waiting for the master to return.

Check in your hands all that he gave you and do business with it. Invest it and trade with it and the master will be happy with you when he returns.

The ECWA theme of the year is urging us to say bye to the era where Christian women sit idly doing no business. Let us say bye to the regime of saying "I am too big to allow my children do business." Look, it is the business men and women that are ruling the world.

Christians must shift their attention to the business world. Government jobs are good but from national experience, it is the salary earner that goes to collect debt from business men/women. No matter how small a business is, in most cases it pays off than some government jobs.

Muslims are found in every nook and cranny of Nigeria selling one thing or the other. Some of them sell goro (kolanut), kwakwa (palm), dabinu (dates), sugarcane, spinach, okra, peppers, onions, meats while some of them even offer house to house services of mending torn clothes, fingernail trimming, shoe shining, etc.

Unfortunately, you will find a Christian who has nothing tangible to show claiming to be too big to involve him/herself in such noble acts. This we must shun if we must occupy the economy of the world for Christ our master. In the village where I come from, there is a spot in the town square called Admin. This place is usually packed full of youth (educated and illiterates) most of whom have no trade.

They sit there to play, argue and spend but never to sell. It is an idle ground for many. In the kind of economy we are, it is injurious for an individual to have no trade. I have no problem with youth spending time in the admin except that they spend time trading nothing. The Admin is the heart of the town where buying and selling will flow.

Today, trade must not even be the sale of physical products to your immediate environment. The admin in Adunu is center of jokes, tough arguments on current issues, sound football analysis and the game of draft is played by experts. Unfortunately, none of this is ever uploaded to the internet

(Youtube, Tiktok, Instagram, etc.) Most of the pile of youth who are regular visitors of admin carry big phones but none of them is seizing the opportunity for business.

Today we are in a world where even laughing attracts followership for a person on the social media. Someone is ready to pay and watch what you are doing that you think is not very important if you upload it to the net. I write and upload books to the internet and they are purchased by people I do not even know.

But Christian youth who are addicted to that place did not care to know how to make an internet business out of their time in the admin neither do they have the wisdom of setting up a bread stand, recharge card outlet, etc.

If we must succeed and become powerful in the economy, then we must not leave trade to non-Christians. We must know how to find a good and quality product of 500 hundred naira and sell it for 600, 700, 800, 900 or even 1000 naira. We must not feel any guilt for doing so. It is called business.

You are not expected to buy a product for 500 naira and sell it at that same price except if you have another way of making a profit from it. As Christians, we must know how to set fair, holy and profitable prices for the goods we purchase or produce for sale. I shall say something a little about this in a latter section.

Lesson 5: **Exclusively Reserved for Servants**

The '*Occupy Till I Come*' is a command given by the master to his servants and for his servants alone. The command and the instruction was not for everyone. It is a command that is intended specifically for the servants of the master – those whom he gave his money to.

The master does not give such a command to those who have not received anything from him. His gifts and resources are strictly for those who are his own. No man who was not among his slaves received any part of the money. The gifts of the master are only for those he called.

In other words, the instruction '*Occupy Till I Come*' is only for and to those of us who are his servants, those who have sincerely embraced the salvation that the Lord Jesus has purchased for us on the cross, and who live consciously in the light of His second coming and the glories that will follow.

We are like those servants in that parable. We are the servants of our Master—the Lord Jesus. We became His servants when He saved us. And then, after He saved us, He poured His grace upon us in a multitude of rich ways.

He washed us clean of our sins and set us free from the past, so that we can go on and live as 'new creations'. This proofs that we are his, the ones he lavished his gifts and resources upon us.

He has declared to us that we now have the right to approach His Father freely, and ask for anything in His own name. He has given us His word—written down for us in Scripture—to be our guide and the rule of our lives. He has given us authority as His ambassadors in this world, and has commissioned us to proclaim His gospel and make disciples.

He has sent the Holy Spirit to take up residence in us, to empower us and 'gift' us for different areas of service to His people. He has promised to provide for all our needs if we will put His kingdom and His righteousness first in our lives.

Bearing all these in mind, he gave us the church a command to invest all that we received from him before he returns.

Lesson 6: Each Servant Was Given a Portion of the Money
The master gave each of the servants a portion of his money. Every one of them received something from the master because the master's resources are meant for his servants.

But to each one of us grace has been given as Christ apportioned it.

No servant was left without a mina. Each of them received a portion of his resources. In a similar way, God has given each of us some minas and we all must use it to bring glory to the master. One thing we share in common is that each of us is given something.

In the first six verses of Ephesians 4, we are called to a life of peace and unity because to each one of us, something is given. While some differences exist among believers, it is in the variety and multiplicity of gifts in the church. But you must know from the text that it is Christ doing, and all such endowments have their part to play in the growth of the whole body.

No matter what God gave you, you must know that God also gave me something too!

Lesson 7: Multiple Streams of Income

The action of the master teaches the need and the wisdom to invest your resources in multiple ventures. This principle is the foundation upon which the proverb "Do not carry all your eggs in one basket" is built. You need more than one source of income. If the source of your income is one, what happens the day some bad luck befalls that one and only source?

The master did not give all his resources into the hands of one man alone. He divided the minas into ten different hands so that if this one fails, the other will not fail. This parable is a timely message for Christians in this dispensation. Principles of investment must be taught on our pulpits, in our Bible studies, Sunday schools, devotional manuals, etc.

Christians' overdependence on government jobs is a big disadvantage. Sometimes around 2020/2021 in Niger state of

Nigeria, the governor ordered all salaries to be slashed. Civil servants were paid a certain percentage of their salaries. Sometimes workers were paid 25% or even 20% of their monthly salaries.

In other words, a person who earns a monthly salary of ₦45,000 was paid ₦11,250 or there about. Many people suffered because salary was their only source of livelihood. To worsen the case, in some months they were not even paid anything and this irregularity in the payment of salary continued for about 2 years. As I write this, some civil servants have not recovered from the shock of those awful months.

The church of God is packed full with men who do not have even one stream of income while some have just one. Only a very few (about 3% by my estimation) knows and applies the wisdom of establishing multiple streams of income.

At such, I feel that giving room for seasoned and reputable Christian investors to teach the Church how to invest the resources in our hands is not carnality. If we must have a say in the economic situation of our countries, then we must spare some of us to become investors. More so, every one of us must have basic knowledge of investing.

For the work of God in our hands to be advanced, resources is required – yes, all kinds of resources. I do believe that we do not need to become beggars on the pulpit but we need to depend on the Holy Spirit to convict men to give. However, what can a man who does not have anything give?

There are men that God have called them to become kingdom financiers, such men must be trained differently. They may not need an intensive training on how to pray for the sick because that is not their area of calling.

The church will need to identify such persons and arrange special Christian investment and business classes for such persons. The parable of the minas is a call into trade, business and investment.

The sectional heading of Ecclesiastes 11:1-6 in the NIV is "Invest in Many Ventures" while the NLT puts it as this "The Uncertainties of Life." That is, you should invest in many ventures due to the uncertainties of life. No matter how careful we are, there are times that the unexpected must always come.

Life is filled with uncertainties. Today, a particular trade may be booming and yielding much profit and the next day, it crashes. Take Soy-Bean as example, in 2021 a measure of it was sold for ₦500 at harvest against the ₦300 it was sold in 2020. Farmers made huge profits from its sale and when the 2022 farming season showed up, every farmer buckled his shoe for the veritable crop.

Many collected loans to enable them cultivate it on a commercial scale and unfortunately, rain was not enough for the crop. So, its yield was very poor. To worsen the situation, the price of Soy-Bean nose-dived from ₦500 per measure to ₦250-300 per measure at the time of my writing. Investors bought it ₦400 - 450 at harvest time for storage only for the price to go astronomically bad.

This is a shocking and sour experience that no one expected, however, no one can change the tide. It is for this kind of unforeseen circumstances that Solomon warned us saying:

[1]Ship your grain across the sea; after many days you may receive a return. [2]Invest in seven ventures, yes, in eight; you do not know what disaster may come upon the land. [6]Sow your seed in the morning, and at evening let your hands not be idle, for you do not know which will succeed, whether this or that, or whether both will do equally well. **NIV**

[1]Be generous: Invest in acts of charity. Charity yields high returns. [2]Don't hoard your goods; spread them around. Be a blessing to others. This could be your last night. [6]Go to work in the morning and stick to it until evening without watching the clock. You never know from moment to moment how your work will turn out in the end. **MSG**

[1]Send your grain across the seas, and in time, profits will flow back to you [2]But divide your investments among many places for you do not know what risks might lie ahead. [6]Plant your seed in the morning and keep busy all

afternoon, for you don't know if profit will come from one activity or another—or maybe both. **NLT**

It is foolishness to invest your resources all in one place for you do not know what risks might lay ahead. Spread your resources around, for you never know from moment to moment how your work will turn out in the end. Invest in different ventures, yes, in more than one venture; for you do not know what disaster may come upon the land. Invest in the morning, and at evening invest, for you do not know which will succeed, whether this or that, or whether both will do equally well.

The application of this principle derived from the verses above helped that master in the parable of the minas a lot. Imagine if he had given all his resources into the hands of that lazy and fearful servant alone, he would have returned to find all his money buried with no profit. This is a lesson, a caution and a warning that we must heed.

For the clergy
As I round up this section on multiple streams of income, I felt it is necessary I lend my voice to a persisting problem that is eating deep into the lives of most clergies. The clergies are those ordained in church: the body of people ordained for religious service, especially in the Christian church.

I want to talk to the pastors, priests and reverends. I am talking to the pastors, priests and reverends who work for church denominations that pay their clergies salaries and have specified a given time period after which their clergies must retire. Take the ECWA for example!

The ECWA denomination has a good priority for the welfare of its serving clergies. Each clergy is paid his salary by the local church he governs and the salary scale is good because it competes favorably with the salary scale of a typical civil servant. Beside this, the pastor is entitled to other benefits.

The local church is urged to offer a token to the family of the clergy during Christmas, New Year and Easter celebrations. The women fellowship is responsible for the provision of firewood to the pastor/reverend's house. They are responsible for the provision of basic soup ingredients like Palm oil, Maggi and Salt for the pastor's wife. I think this is good enough!

It is the duty of the local church to organize a farm labor to assist the clergy at least once in a farming season! Where any of these cannot be practically done by the local church, it is monetized (I.e. the local church provides all the money needed to get these things done). I am saying what I know is done to clergies of churches like COCIN, ECWA, etc.

Yet, I have come across retired clergies who looked pitiful and lived beggarly after using 35 years of their lives to serve at the honorable altar of our Lord Jesus Christ. Reverends and pastors who were chubby and plump while they serve as pastors of local churches soon became lean and slender like the lean cows of Pharaoh's dream.

This is true of most clergies in the urban and rural areas and it is already becoming a norm that most retire clergies must end poor and live miserable lives afterwards. I kept wondering what likely could be the cause of this kind of an ending. Why are clergies miserable after retirement? Why can't they afford their hospital bills after they retire? Why do they keep coming back to the local churches to request for help after their retirement?

This I wondered and out of the so many possible causes I self-evaluated, the lack of multiple streams of income is the grand chief of all. The problem is mustered by a sole dependence of most clergies on salary and donations from the local churches. It is a problem that is common to most salary earners in and out of the church.

The clergies are humans like any other person. They too are not immune from the realities of life. Ordination does not give anyone the prerogative to ignore basic life principles of investment. If you follow them, you succeed; refuse to follow them and you fail.

The sad ending of many clergies cannot be blamed on God. Following God does not mean you should fail to make provision for your future, your retirement and life outside the local church. If you do not have a common hut to move into after your retirement, it is your fault and not the fault of your call.

Most clergies depend on salary and salary alone. Until recently when I noticed one clergy (Pastor Amos Tukura) selling Christian literatures and Bibles, I used to think that part of the oath taken by the clergies includes an embargo against trade, investments and business. But this is not so.

This attitude by some clergies is due to ignorance and pride. I am not saying that clergies should forsake their primary assignment and go to find money. No! Neither am I against the welfare provisions enjoyed by the clergies from their local churches.

What I am saying is this, "After serving and earning some money for 35 years, you ought not to become very miserable. As a serving clergy, you must plan not to become like those who became miserable after their retirement. You must push part of all you are now earning for investment. While you are now earning salary, you must get an extra source of income so that even if your clerical salary stops today, you will still have a way of getting some income."

It is never God's plan for his servants to end miserably. Learn from Apostle Paul who combined ministry work with tent making. Tent making was a menial job that will not deny him full concentration on the work God gave him. Paul was entitled to receiving basic supplies and provisions from the people he ministered to. Yet, he engaged himself in the business of making and selling tents. Acts 18:1-3.

For this reason, as a clergy who is paid salary, what "tent making" enterprise are you engaged in?

Lesson 8: **From One Source**

All the *minas* came from one source to all of them. The *minas* were all given by the master. He alone is the distributor of the *minas*. Any *mina* owned by his servants came from him. None of the servants got his *minas* from somewhere else. We all have received from one and the same source.

Though many servants, they all have one master. We are many servants but we have one master. All our gifts and the resources we obtained are from the same source. For this reason, we must make every effort to keep the unity of the Spirit through the bond of peace.

There is one body and one Spirit, just as you were called to one hope when you were called; one Lord, one faith, one baptism; one God and Father of all, who is over all and through all and in all.

There are many things we share in common: we share a common Lord and master; we share a common treasure – *minas*. No one's gifts are better. You were given the same *minas* I was given, you were not given gold while I received silver. All our gifts are from the same source and are made of the same quality. So your own possession from the Lord is not superior to mine. At most, your gifts will only be different from mine in quantity and this is determined by the chief distributor alone – the Holy Spirit.

There may be difference in the amount we each received but we are all given of the same thing. No fight must break out among us. We need to be strongly united and form strong business alliance as partners. If we collaborate and form strong business synergies, we will succeed.

We must work together, join forces, team up, work in partnership, pool resources, act as a team and cooperate with one another. There is no need to be jealous of anyone because whatever profit each one of us is making is for the master, our one and only master – Jesus Christ.

It is pathetic today that Christians are fighting among themselves. Any kingdom divided against it-self shall not stand. We fight over church members; we fight and compete with each other over lands, positions, etc. we forget that whatever anyone has among us is for our dear master who gave us the charge to "*Occupy till he comes.*"

In other words, whatever space and sphere of life anyone occupies is not for him/her-self. He/she is just holding it up for the master who is the real owner. We are just ambassadors and stewards. The real owner will soon be back. This we must take note.

Lesson 9: **The Master Will Surely Return**
*'Trade with this money until **I come back**.'*

"He was made king, however, and returned home"

In the instruction *'Trade with this money until I come back,'* the master promised his servants that he will return, that he will come back to them. The master told them he will travel away but he was not going to stay there forever.

If the master will remain there forever, the behaviour of his disciples will be different. Knowing that he will return calls for carefulness, diligence and caution.

If the master will not return, it will mean there will be no need for reckoning. The master will certainly come back. His return is definite and sure. It may take too long but he will surely come back.

The Lord is not slow in keeping to the promise of his return, as some understand slowness. Instead he is patient with you, not wanting anyone to perish, but everyone to come to repentance. [4]

There are some who thinks the master's promise to return is not true. They think it has taking too long, about two thousand years. They are saying the master is slow, and even conclude that he may not return. This kind of thought is evil in itself as it so paints our dear master to be a liar.

---

[4] 2Peter 3:9 (NIV)

But this promise cannot be a lie "*If I go and prepare a place for you, I will come back and take you to be with me that you also may be where I am.*"[5]

The master will surely return, we (his servants) must take caution to use all the resources that he gave us in a way that agrees with his own terms.

The day of reckoning is coming when we each must stand before the master to give an account of how he used the gifts, blessings and talents that he gave us.

[10]Each of you should use whatever gift you have received to serve others, as faithful stewards of God's grace in its various forms. [11]If anyone speaks, they should do so as one who speaks the very words of God. If anyone serves, they should do so with the strength God provides, so that in all things God may be praised through Jesus Christ. To him be the glory and the power for ever and ever. Amen.

Beloved, while waiting for the second return of the Lord Jesus to subjugate or quash every rebellion against His authority and establish His everlasting physical Kingdom on earth, the Lord expects you to occupy or do business till He comes.

---

[5] John 14:3 (NLT)

Wherever the Lord has placed or positioned you, it is His Lord's expectation that you will continue His ministry, proclaim and demonstrate his Lordship and His preeminence. (John 17:18, 20:21).

As a believer, you are not supposed to be waiting passively for the return of the Lord Jesus, but to be laboring actively in God's kingdom, bearing much fruit from the grace you have received from the Lord Jesus.

Apostle Paul admonishes us saying, "*We then, as workers together with Him also plead with you not to receive the grace of God in vain.*" (2 Cor. 6:1 NKJV).

When you fail to labour diligently or actively towards the growth and expansion of God's kingdom on earth, you have simply received the grace of God in vain.

Lesson 9: The Day of Reckoning

15 Then he sent for the servants to whom he had given the money, in order to find out what they had gained with it.

17 For it is time for judgment to begin with God's household; and if it begins with us, what will the outcome be for those who do not obey the gospel of God? 18 And,

"If it is hard for the righteous to be saved, what will become of the ungodly and the sinner?"[6]

From the parable, you will understand that when the master returned, he first of all called his own servants in order to find out what they had gained with the money he gave them. Judgement first began with his own servants and afterwards his enemies.

Peter later confirmed that the sequence of events in the parable is the very template of how God will address the world when Jesus returns. Account will be required from the servants and the punishment of the avowed enemies of Christ, as well as of false professors, is shown.

The Rapture

I intend to say something brief about rapture because I am talking to you about the return of the master – permit me to say the second coming of Christ. The word *"rapture"* means

- An overwhelming happiness: a euphoric transcendent state in which somebody is overwhelmed by happiness or delight and unaware of anything else.

- A mystical transportation in Christianity: a mystical experience in which somebody believes he or she is transported into the spiritual realm, sometimes applied

---

[6] 1 Peter 4:17

to the second coming of Jesus Christ, when true believers are expected to rise up to join him in heaven[7]

The second meaning is intended here. The word rapture is not found in the entire scripture. However, reference to the term is found in descriptive form throughout the entire bible.

As stated above, rapture is defined in the words found in the book of Revelation 1:7 *"Look, he is coming with the clouds," and "every eye will see him, even those who pierced him"; and all peoples on earth "will mourn because of him." So shall it be! Amen.*

This is the best and simplest definition of rapture. It is the return of Jesus Christ with the clouds to come and take his servants to the place he prepared for them. All the peoples of the earth will mourn when they see him coming with the clouds of heaven, with power and great glory.

The master will send his angels with a loud trumpet call, and they will gather his elect from the four winds of the earth, from one end of the heavens to the other. This is rapture!

Christians are not left in the dark regarding the rapture. Its meaning, how it will occur, when it will occur, what must happen before it occurs, the antichrist, the great tribulation, and

---

[7] Microsoft® Encarta® 2009. © 1993-2008 Microsoft Corporation. All rights reserved.

every single event that is connected to the return of the master is explained in the scriptures.

When Will He Return?

As regards when this will happen, Jesus told us this:

1. *No one knows the exact day or hour when these things will happen. Not even the angels in heaven or the Son himself. Only the Father knows.*

2. *His return, will be like it was in Noah's day*

3. *In those days before the flood, the people were enjoying banquets and parties and weddings right up to the time Noah entered his boat.*

4. *People didn't realize what was going to happen until the flood came and swept them all away. That is the way it will be when the Son of Man comes.*[8]

---

[8] Matthew 24:36-39

5. *"You also must be ready, because the Son of Man will come at an hour when you do not expect him."[9]*

Of course, no one knows the exact day that Christ will return. All those who ever predicted it failed. It is heresy to predict Christ's second coming. We have no business trying to find out the exact day when the master will show up to take us into glory.

However, Jesus did gave us clues of events that must signal the nearness of his return.

1. *"For many will come in my name, claiming, 'I am the Messiah,' and will deceive many.*
2. *You will hear of wars and rumors of wars.*

3. *Such things must happen, but the end is still to come.*

4. *Nation will rise against nation, and kingdom against kingdom.*

5. *There will be famines and earthquakes in various places.*

---

[9] Luke 12:40

6. *All these are the beginning of birth pains.*

7. *"Then you will be handed over to be persecuted and put to death, and you will be hated by all nations because of me.*

8. *At that time many will turn away from the faith and will betray and hate each other,*

9. *Many false prophets will appear and deceive many people.*

10. *Wickedness will increase*

11. *The love of many people will grow cold.*

12. *The gospel of the kingdom will be preached in the whole world as a testimony to all nations, and then the end will come.*

13. *The abomination that causes desolation spoken of through the prophet Daniel would be seeing standing in the holy place.*

14. *Those days will be dreadful for pregnant women and nursing mothers!*

15. *For then there will be great distress, unequaled from the beginning of the world until now—and never to be equaled again.*

16. *Those days will be shortened to enable the elect survive. "If those days had not been cut short, no one would survive.*

17. *Some deceivers will come and say 'Look, here is the Messiah!' or, 'There he is!'*

18. *False messiahs and false prophets will appear and perform great signs and wonders to deceive, if possible, even the elect.*

19. *"Immediately after the distress of those days " 'the sun will be darkened, and the moon will not give its light; the stars will fall from the sky, and the heavenly bodies will be shaken.*

20. *Even so, when you see all these things, you know that it is near, right at the door.*

21. *"It is not for you to know the times or dates the Father has set by his own authority.*[10]

All these above must happen to signal the nearness of the master's return. *"Then will appear the sign of the Son of Man in heaven."*

"So if anyone tells you, 'There he is, out in the wilderness,' do not go out; or, 'Here he is, in the inner rooms,' do not believe it. For as lightning that comes from the east is visible even in the west, so will be the coming of the Son of Man."[11]

How Will It Occur?

Our master indeed travelled. He is currently away but he will be back. However, it is important I point out to you that it is not some earthly country that he travelled to. It is not Dubai or Switzerland that he went to.

So it will be good to settle it in our hearts that the master we are waiting for will not return on an airplane and definitely not in a car. He will return by the same means he left.

---

[10] Acts 1:7
[11] Matthew 24:26-27

Jesus was taken up into the cloud while his disciples were watching. And as they strained to see him ascend into heaven, two white-robed men suddenly stood among them and said to them

> *"Men of Galilee, why are you standing here staring into heaven? Jesus has been taken from you into heaven, but someday **he will return from heaven in the same way you saw him go!**"*[12]

The master's return will be like this: The master himself will come down from heaven, with a loud command, with the voice of the archangel and with the trumpet call of God, and his servants that are dead will resurrect from the dead and rise first to meet him in the sky.

After that, we (his servants) who are still alive and are left will be caught up together with them in the clouds to meet the Lord (our master) in the air. And so we will be with the Lord forever. There are heavenly bodies and there are also earthly bodies. The glory of the heavenly bodies is different from the glory of the earthly bodies.

It is the same way with the resurrection of the dead. Our bodies are buried in brokenness, but they will be raised in glory. They are buried as natural human bodies, but they will be raised as spiritual bodies. For just as there are natural bodies, there are also spiritual bodies.

---

[12] Acts 1

What comes first is the natural body, then the spiritual body comes later. Our physical bodies cannot inherit the Kingdom of God. These dying bodies cannot inherit what will last forever. A wonderful secret is this: *"Not all servants of the master will die before his return for some of them will still be alive when he returns but they cannot meet him with this physical body and so, they will all be transformed!"*

The bodies of his servants that will still be alive then, shall be changed just as his servants that are dead will put on new spiritual bodies. It will all happen in a moment, in the blink of an eye, when the last trumpet is blown.

For when the trumpet sounds, those who have died will be raised to live forever. And we who are living will also be transformed. For our dying bodies must be transformed into bodies that will never die; our mortal bodies must be transformed into immortal bodies.

Only the dead will resurrect. The living are not dead, so they will not experience resurrection but their bodies will indeed be transformed. At the coming of Jesus Christ, only his servants that are dead will resurrect. However, the dead who are not his servants will also resurrect later but unto eternal condemnation.[13]

---

[13] Daniel12:2 Multitudes who sleep in the dust of the earth will awake: some to everlasting life, others to shame and everlasting contempt.

Lesson 10: Fear Cripples

*[20]"But the third servant brought back only the original amount of money and said, 'Master, I hid your money and kept it safe. [21]I was **afraid** because you are a hard man to deal with, taking what isn't yours and harvesting crops you didn't plant.'*

The unfaithful servant did not invest his master's money because he was afraid. He was afraid of losing his mater's money, so he hid the money.

So for the time being when his master was away, he was either idle or busybody. He was either idle (sleeping or watching film) all day or he was busy helping his friends to do business with their own money while failing to engage his own resources in business due to fear.

So many people are kept from reaching their full potential because of fear. They are afraid of trying something new and so, they maintain status quo. They bury their *mina*, bury their potentials. Fear makes people to play it safe. It keeps men from thinking outside the box. Fear of failure is a great hindrance to maximizing potential.

They may not be lazy people because they may want to work but fear drags them down and so, they lazy around. The lazy person claims, *"There's a lion on the road! Yes, I'm sure there's a lion out there!"*

As a door swings back and forth on its hinges, so the lazy person turns over in bed and bury his head in his blanket. Lazy people take food in their hand but don't even lift it to their mouth.[14]

In other words, a person can fail to maximize some opportunities due to fear. In the face of a clean opportunity in business or even in ministry, fear of failure will convince such a person that there is a lion in the way to that opportunity. And that is how the person will refuse to attempt that until the opportunity passes.

All life's opportunities are embedded and packaged as risks. Nothing significant can be achieved in life without risk taking. The greater the risk, the greater the reward; so, do not be afraid to take risks. The Message paraphrased the master's words in Luke 19:26 this way,

> The Master said, *'That's what I mean: Risk your life and get more than you ever dreamed of. Play it safe and end up holding the bag.* Luke 19:26 MSG

Fearful people may wish to step out but they do not have the guts to adventure into that which God is calling them into.

---

14 Proverbs 26:13

They do not know that the master will only instruct you to do what he has furnished you for. Because for every task he gives you, he gives you commensurate resources and the enablement needed to fulfill it.

If you wish to know the kind of grace, anointing, gifts and abilities that the master gives you, then check the assignment he is given you. The assignment God will give you is usually and always compatible to the gifts he has given you. His assignment for you is an indicator of your gifts, talents and abilities.

There are many Christians who wish to start one business or the other but they are afraid of trying. The fear that they might lose their capital, that there are many competitors and so, they shrink back. God has not given us the spirit of fear but of power, love and of a sound mind.

If your heart moves you to do something and the Holy Spirit does not object it, please go ahead. Overcome your fears and step out in faith. The master knows that you could lose it but yet, he asked you to trade with the resources he gave you.

Can you imagine the different instances that fear kept you from maximizing some opportunities?

Lesson 11: **The Master Has Enemies**

"But the citizens there hated him. So they sent a commission with a signed petition to oppose his rule: 'We don't want this man to rule us.' MSG*

"But those enemies of mine who did not want me to be king over them—bring them here and kill them in front of me."

"For it is time for judgment to begin with God's household; and if it begins with us, what will the outcome be for those who do not obey the gospel of God? [18]And, "If it is hard for the righteous to be saved, what will become of the ungodly and the sinner?"

The country is not only composed of the servants of the master. There are some other citizens of that country who refuse to submit to his leadership. In fact, when he was away to receive full authority, they send a delegation to register their petition against his kingship.

The master had and still has enemies today. There are many people on earth who still refuse to become servants of the master, - Jesus Christ the righteous one. They hate to have the master become their Lord.

They are the antichrists and many of them have come into the world. Important to note is that the servants of the master are living in the same world and country with the enemies of the master. These enemies of the master mock his servants and maltreat them.

They try hard enough to place obstacles and persuade the master's servants to refuse the yoke of the master. The master is aware of these enemies and has plans in place of how to handle them. These enemies will not go scot free. Eternal punishment quite awaits them.

They are enemies of Christ who are even in the church with us. They went out from us but they really did not belong to us.

These wolves in sheep's clothing infiltrated our ranks. But beneath their pious skin are shameless scoundrels. Their design is to replace the sheer grace of our God with sheer license—which means doing away with Jesus Christ, our one and only Master.[15]

- Some of them will pretend to be friends and seek to deceive us while

- Some of them will not hide their hatred against our master. They will show up their anger and kill us, make us to suffer and deny us certain rights and privileges.

Jesus knew that his enemies are automatically the enemies of his servants. He knew they will transfer their anger and hatred for him to his servants. That is why he told us beforehand that:

---

[15] Jude 1:4

- *Blessed are those who are persecuted because of righteousness, for theirs is the kingdom of heaven.*

Meaning his enemies will persecute us (his servants) in life

- *"Blessed are you when people insult you, persecute you and falsely say all kinds of evil against you because of me."* [16]

For the sake of the master, his servants will suffer some difficulties and maltreatment from the enemies of their master.

The enemies of the master are automatically critics of his servants. If a master who empowered his servants with business capital can be petitioned then what good thing can any servant do without criticism?

- *Rejoice and be glad, because great is your reward in heaven, for in the same way they persecuted the prophets who were before you.*

The terrible treatment that the servants of the master will receive will be duly rewarded in the life to come.

---

[16] Matthew 6

- *Blessed are you when people hate you, when they exclude you and insult you and reject your name as evil, because of the Son of Man. "Rejoice in that day and leap for joy, because great is your reward in heaven. For that is how their ancestors treated the prophets.*

The enemies of the master will not spare his servants. They will hate and insult his servants. If the servants of the master apply for anything (admission, scholarship, grants or employment) in the civil service, their names would be excluded and rejected by these enemies. However, the servants of the master are told by the master himself that this should never become a problem to us because we shall be adequately compensated in heaven.

- *Love your enemies, do good to those who hate you, bless those who curse you, pray for those who mistreat you.*

It is the duty of the servants of the master to love, do good to, bless and pray for these enemies that that hates, curse, maltreats them. What a difficult game!

- *If someone slaps you on one cheek, turn to them the other also. If someone takes your coat, do not withhold your shirt from them.*

The servants of the master will be slapped and unjustly robbed of their possessions on earth by these enemies.

- *Give to everyone who asks you, and if anyone takes what belongs to you, do not demand it back. Love your enemies, do good to them, and lend to them without expecting to get anything back. Then your reward will be great, and you will be children of the Most High, because he is kind to the ungrateful and wicked.*
The servants of the master are not permitted in any way to also hate the enemies of the master.[17]

- *Surely, since I, the master of the household, have been called the prince of demons (Beelzebub) the members of my household will be called by even worse names! "But don't be afraid of those who threaten you.[18]*

---

[17] Luke 6
[18] Matthew 10:25

Note: While the master has many enemies, he has only one arch enemy. All the other enemies are subordinates of the arch enemy – the antichrist. His name antichrist is coined from two words *Anti* = against and *Christ* = The Messiah, the master.

Therefore his name clearly reveals who he is. He is against Christ, he do not want Christ to reign over him and will do everything possible to ensure that.

Not only will he refuse the reign of Christ, he will persuade and force the whole world to include their names in the petition list against the master.

First John tells us that many antichrists have come into the world. These are all people, anyone who is against Christ and makes a deliberate effort to keep people from knowing and accepting the reign of Christ.

However, among all the enemies of Christ, there is a chief. He is "The Antichrist". Paul in the book of 2 Thessalonians gave this revelation:

Events prior to the Lord's Second Coming
¹Now, dear brothers and sisters, let us clarify some things about the coming of our Lord Jesus Christ and how we will be gathered to meet him. ²Don't be so easily shaken or alarmed by those who say that the day of the Lord has already begun. Don't believe them, even if they

claim to have had a spiritual vision, a revelation, or a letter supposedly from us.

³Don't be fooled by what they say. For that day will not come until there is a great rebellion against God and the man of lawlessness is revealed—the one who brings destruction. ⁴He will exalt himself and defy everything that people call god and every object of worship. He will even sit in the temple of God, claiming that he himself is God.

⁵Don't you remember that I told you about all this when I was with you? ⁶And you know what is holding him back, for he can be revealed only when his time comes. ⁷For this lawlessness is already at work secretly and it will remain secret until the one who is holding it back steps out of the way.

⁸Then the man of lawlessness will be revealed, but the Lord Jesus will kill him with the breath of his mouth and destroy him by the splendor of his coming. ⁹This man will come to do the work of Satan with counterfeit power and signs and miracles.

¹⁰He will use every kind of evil deception to fool those on their way to destruction, because they refuse to love

and accept the truth that would save them. *11So God will cause them to be greatly deceived, and they will believe these lies.*

12Then they will be condemned for enjoying evil rather than believing the truth.

The antichrist is the little horn of the book of Daniel and the beast of the book of Revelation 13. This little horn will persecute the saints and force men to accept the mark of the beast on their foreheads or on their right hand.

No one can buy or sell unless they had the mark, which is the name of the beast or the number of its name. This calls for wisdom. Let the person who has insight calculate the number of the beast, for it is the number of a man. That number is 666.

Lesson 12: This is just the Tidbit
17" 'Well done, my good servant!' his master replied. 'Because you have been trustworthy in a very small matter, take charge of ten cities.'

The seemingly huge sum of money the master gave to his servants was just a test. It is just a tidbit of what the master had in store for his servants. The servants who deal faithfully with what they were given were given more responsibilities and resources. They were promoted to govern cities, one five cities, the other three cities.

The one who did not engage what he was given in business was not given any more responsibility. In fact, what he had was seized and given to those who trade with their resources. In other words, whatever the master is given us now is just a test that will determine whether or not the master will usher us into something great.

The parable reveals to us that what Christ will lavish on us when he returns will far surpass all that he now gave us. *When Christ, who is your life, appears, then you also will appear with him in glory.* Colossians 3:4

But I do not want you to only be heavenly minded. I want you to know that faithfulness with the master's responsibilities also holds earthly benefits for us. Physical training has some value, but godliness has value for all things, holding promise for both the present life (on earth) and the life to come (in heaven).

This should not be argued by anyone because it is a trustworthy saying that deserves full acceptance. So, let us labor and strive, as we have put our hope in the living God, who is the Savior of all people, and especially of those who believe. Let us command and teach believers to use, invest, trade, do business and make profit with whatever God places in our care.

The little we now hold is just very little of what he will usher us into in the days to come. All that God has given us is just the tidbit of the main thing.

SECTION C
TRADE

4

Trade

The etymology of the word *Trade* reveals that "Trade" is from Middle English trade ("path, course of conduct"), introduced into English by Hanseatic merchants, from Middle Low German trade ("track, course"), from Old Saxon trada ("spoor, track"), from Proto-Germanic "tradō" ("track, way"), and cognate with Old English tredan ("to tread").

The word *Trade* originated from human communication in prehistoric times. Trading was the main facility of prehistoric people who exchanged goods and services from each other in a gift economy before the innovation of modern-day currency.

Trade is believed to have taken place throughout much of recorded human history. There is evidence of the exchange of *obsidian* and flint during the Stone Age. Trade in obsidian is believed to have taken place in New Guinea from 17,000 BCE.

Trade is believed to have first begun in south west Asia. Archaeological evidence of the use of *obsidian* provides data on how this material was increasingly the preferred choice rather than *chert* from the late Mesolithic to Neolithic, requiring exchange as deposits of *obsidian* are rare in the Mediterranean region.

Obsidian is thought to have provided the material to make cutting utensils or tools, although since other more easily obtainable materials were available, use was found exclusive to the higher status of the tribe using "the rich man's flint". Interestingly, *Obsidian* has held its value relative to flint.

In ancient Greece *Hermes* was the god of trade (commerce) and weights and measures. In ancient Rome, *Mercurius* was the god of merchants, whose festival was celebrated by traders on the 25th day of the fifth month. It therefore means that trade is a major aspect of life that we need to pay careful attention to.

As a verb, the word *trade* is synonymous to the following words:

- Deal, buy and sell, do business, operate, traffic, import, export, merchandize, transact

- Exchange, swap, barter, dicker (*informal*), negotiate[19]

Trade involves the transfer of goods and services from one person or entity to another, often in exchange for money today. Economists refer to a system or network that allows trade as a **market**.

---

[19] Microsoft® Encarta® 2009. © 1993-2008 Microsoft Corporation.

An early form of trade, **barter**, saw the direct exchange of goods and services for other goods and services, i.e. trading things without the use of money.

However, today modern traders generally negotiate through a medium of exchange, such as money. As a result, buying can be separated from selling, or earning. The invention of money (and letter of credit, paper money, and non-physical money) greatly simplified and promoted trade.

In trade, the ownership of goods or services is transferred from one person to the other in consideration of cash or cash equivalents. Trade between two traders is called **bilateral trade**, while trade involving more than two traders is called **multilateral trade**.

A person who trades is called a **trader** and different types of traders may specialize in trading different kinds of goods. This is very necessary because every type of trader is important.

For example, the sugarcane trader and grain trader have both historically been important in the development of a global, international economy.

So, what that master told his servants to trade with the money until he returns can be paraphrased as:

- Buy and sell with this money until I return

- Import and/or export goods and services with this money until I return

- Do business negotiations and transactions with this money till I returnU

- Do not be idle but become merchants with this money till I return.

Jesus then reveals that his followers are free to do business with the resources he placed in their hands. Islamic teachings encourage trading (and condemn usury or interest). Judeao-Christian teachings do not prohibit trade.

Virtually all religions of the world did not forbid trading because except if done unjustly, trading is a sanctimonious aspect of human life. However, they do prohibit fraud and dishonest measures.

By this parable, Jesus charged his servants to do business, to trade and to be involved in commerce. Trade shapes the world. The strength of a nation's trade determines its gross income. The most powerful people on earth are traders (business men).

Aliko Dangote, Bill Gates, Elon Musk, Steve Jobs, Mark Zukerberg, Donald Trump, Robert Kiyosaki and even the Bush family are all traders in a sense. These men among the powerful men of our generation and it is trade that gave them such a strong stand.

The master does not want his servants to be only involved with house chores. Beside keeping their master's house, they are to be involved in the day to day economy activities of business.

Forms of Trade

```
                        ┌──────────┐
                        │  Trade   │
                        └──────────┘
             ┌───────────────┴───────────────┐
      ┌──────────────┐                 ┌──────────────┐
      │    Home      │                 │   Foreign    │
      │    Trade     │                 │    Trade     │
      └──────────────┘                 └──────────────┘
       ┌──────┴──────┐         ┌────────────┼────────────┐
┌───────────┐ ┌───────────┐ ┌──────────┐ ┌──────────┐ ┌──────────┐
│ Wholesale │ │  Retail   │ │  Import  │ │  Export  │ │ Entrepot │
│   Trade   │ │   Trade   │ │  Trade   │ │  Trade   │ │  Trade   │
└───────────┘ └───────────┘ └──────────┘ └──────────┘ └──────────┘
```

For the ECWA denomination this year 2023 is an important year to stress and emphasize the importance of business, trading, investment, etc. ECWA pulpits must become platforms that will muster awareness campaigns on the need for Christians to learn and do business at different levels.

Christians have long been drenched in this stupor of not doing business. Christians are chasers of "white collar jobs" which are nowhere to be found. This theme is an opportunity for all clergies to encourage Christians to engage in business. Each one of us must have a side trade to back up what he is doing because traders/investors rule the world.

We must know that there are many forms of trade. We must not think of only the woman who sells fried groundnut by the road side when we talk of trade. The person who goes to China to buy and bring goods into Nigeria is also trading.

Trade can be classified as domestic as well as foreign.

1. **Home/Domestic trade** is the trade within the border of a country. This form of trade is split into:

   a. **Retail trade** consists of the sale of goods or merchandise from a very fixed location (such as a department store, boutique or kiosk), online or by mail, in small or individual lots for direct consumption or use by the purchaser.

   A retail trader is a link between Wholesaler and consumers. Retailers buy products in less quantity from the wholesalers and sell the products to the consumers as per their needs.

   The Retailer is the person who brings the products to consumers. Small-scale retailers include hawkers, peddlers, general shops, etc..

   b. **Wholesale trade** is traffic in goods that are sold as merchandise to retailers, or to industrial, commercial, institutional, or other professional business users, or to other wholesalers and related subordinated services.

It is the trade a wholesaler buys goods in large quantity from the manufacturer and sells them to the retailer. A wholesaler is the intermediary between the manufacturer and the retailer.

A scriptural example of someone who practiced this kind of trade is Lydia the mother of Mark. Lydia was a dealer (bought and sold) in purple cloth. She was a worshiper of God. Naomi Mainasara is our contemporary example of a Christian woman who deals in clothing business.

Wholesaler is a link between producers and retailer. The wholesaler buys the products in large quantities from Manufacturers and sale to retailer and retailer sell to the consumers. A wholesaler acts as an intermediary between producers and retailers.

2. **Foreign trade** is trade across the borders. It is done between one or more countries. Foreign trade is done through investment in securities or funds and can be grouped as imports and exports.

It is the exchange of goods and services across national borders. In most countries, it represents a significant part of GDP.

International trade has been present throughout much of history and its economic, social, and political importance have increased in recent centuries, mainly because of Industrialization, advanced transportation, globalization, multinational corporations, and outsourcing.

a. **Import Trade** refers to the process when a home country obtains or purchase goods from another country for its personal use.

In import trade, a trader of any country buys the products from another country's trader. For example, a trader from Nigeria purchases goods from a trader in China to sell them in Nigeria.

*Solomon the king had horses. These horses were **imported** from Egypt and from Cilicia; the king's traders acquired them from Cilicia at the standard price. At that time chariots from Egypt could be purchased for 600 pieces of silver, and horses for 150 pieces of silver. They were then **exported** to* *the kings of the Hittites and the kings of Aram.[20]*

b. **Export Trade** is when a country sells their products to another country. For example, a trader from Nigeria sells his goods to a trader located in Nairobi Kenya.

c. **Entrepot Trade** means when one country import products from one country and then re-export the products to another country after adding some values.

An example of such is if a Nigerian imports Nike shoes from Dubai and repackage them into a very beautiful casing and export them to Niger.

This was the kind of trade practiced by Solomon.

Free Trade

Free trade is a policy by which a government does not discriminate against imports or exports by applying tariffs or subsidies. This policy is also known as laissez-faire policy.

---

[20] 2 Chronicles 1:16-17

This kind of policy does not necessarily imply that because of it, a country will then abandon all control and taxation of imports and exports.

As believers, we must know the laws governing trade in our country. There are certain goods you can import or even export, this you must know. Because if you import goods without a free trade policy, they goods will be confiscated by government agencies: NAFDAC, Nigerian Custom Service, etc.

Protectionism

Protectionism is the policy of restraining and discouraging trade between states and contrasts with the policy of free trade. This policy often takes the form of tariffs and restrictive quotas. Protectionist policies were particularly prevalent in the 1930s, between the Great Depression and the onset of World War II.

This was practiced in Nigeria when President Muhammadu Buhari banned the importation of some goods into Nigeria. For example; importation of foreign rice was banned in 2019.

Trade Sanctions

Trade sanctions are embargos externally imposed on a nation in order to punish that country for some action.

An embargo, a severe form of externally imposed isolation, is a blockade of all trade by one country on another. For example, the United States has had an embargo against Cuba for over 40 years.

Embargoes are usually on a temporary basis. For example, Armenia put a temporary embargo on Turkish products and bans any imports from Turkey on December 31, 2020.

The situation is prompted by food security concerns given Turkey's hostile attitude towards Armenia.

Advantages of Trade (doing business)

1. Growth Of The Economy

Trade Provide growth to the economy because when trade starts in any country it brings new opportunities to people which also bring money in public. So, trade is the most important pillar for the growth of any economy.

2. Provides Global Presence

When a country starts trading in domestic and International market, global reach is started automatically because the people of other countries will start buying the product. So, trade provides global presence to the economy.

3. Helps In Civilizations

When trade starts in any country it helps in improving personal growth of the people because trade runs in a systematic way.

So, when trade starts it does not only give to the people it also teach them administrations.

4. Provide High Quality Products

When trade starts it brings high compositions as well. When the compositions come in, monopoly of the products is removed. Lastly, when trade starts it provide high quality products to the consumers.

5. Trade Improves Financial Performance

Once trade begins it starts providing tax to the governments. This allows them to augment the returns they achieve on their investments into research and development.

6. Maximum Utilization Of Natural Resources

Trade helps each country to utilize their natural resources in effective ways to produce high-quality products at the cheapest rate. Wastage of resources automatically reduces because once trade starts it brings high skilled employees.

7. Trade Encourages Market Competition

When more brands come into the market competitions increase and that gives more options and quality to the consumers at a low price and remove monopoly.

8. Trade Develops Sympathies

Trade develops sympathies and creates common interests between trading country. It also exchanges the ideas traditions, customs. This promotes international understanding and peace among the people. If war starts it can be remove by people's love and understanding.

When trade starts it does not only provide goods and services to the home country alone but also exports these to other countries.

9. Increase In Efficiency

Trade helps a country to increase their productivity because trade brings high productivity machine and best technology to the host country. This increases the efficiency and benefits to the consumers all over the world.

Entrepreneurs

Entrepreneurs are not only provided with opportunities that benefit themselves, but their work also develops the economy.

1. Entrepreneurs provide job opportunities

One of the main reasons why individuals tend to become entrepreneurs is because they are unable to find suitable jobs. Entrepreneurs create new businesses and in turn create opportunities of employment for people.

Starting a business is an opportunity to either work for themselves or they can help support and develop an entrepreneur's business. Not only are entrepreneurs able to generate an income for themselves but they also employ other individuals in their business operations.

Therefore, people who did not have a job before will have a chance to have a career.

2.   Entrepreneurs increase competition & boost productivity
Entrepreneurs challenge existing firms to become more competitive as they often enter the market with lower prices and greater product variety.

This can cause existing players in the market to re-assess their operations, increase their value, lower costs, and become more efficient.

Increased competition in an economy is advantageous because firms and individuals will source methods to better improve their operations. The new business formation of entrepreneurs with high-growth ambitions and innovation will push established firms to increase their productivity and enhance their performance.

3.   Entrepreneurs create new business & new markets
As the trends in the world continue to change, people's demands will change, giving entrepreneurs an opportunity to start new businesses.

If a marketplace is saturated, this can result in entrepreneurs seeking new markets for their services and products, which can be considered as a positive impact on the economy. Entrepreneurs may even create entirely new industries that become the engines of future growth.

4.   Entrepreneurs add national income

The new products or services created by entrepreneurs result in new wealth from the new markets. Additionally, higher earnings due to entrepreneurship can help boost national income. This is in the form of higher government spending and tax revenue, resulting in investment in struggling sectors and human capital.

5.   Entrepreneurs introduce innovative technologies
Individuals often resort to entrepreneurship to provide niche solutions or to use their creativity, technological knowledge, or finances to generate their own income. Innovative ideas and inventiveness are foundational driving factors for entrepreneurs which result in great contribution to the economy.

Like some of the legendary names in business, Bill Gates (Microsoft), Larry Ellison (Oracle), Steve Jobs (Apple) and many more, entrepreneurs create innovations. New and improved products enable new markets which often lead to economic growth.[21]

Major benefits of business in the local economy
Major benefits of business in the local economy include a boost in employment and discretionary income in the

[21] The Advantages of Businesses in the Local Economy By David Ingram Updated Accessed February 05, 2019

community, tax income increases for local governments and a loyal customer base for businesses.

A. Local Employment and Income

One of the most personal advantages of businesses in the local economy is the boost in employment in the region. Employment levels influence a range of other standard-of-living metrics, such as disposable income, home foreclosure rates and new small business startups.

Employing people in the local community can stimulate word-of-mouth advertising for a company as well, assuming the company treats its employees well enough to get positive mentions. Local employment also cultivates a sense of community, which can enhance the brand of a local business.

B. Local Tax Income

Businesses pay a significant portion of taxes to the government, including income tax, property tax and employment tax.

Having more businesses in the local economy can boost tax income for local governments, bringing in more money to repair roads, develop schools and improve public services.

The weight of the gold that Solomon received yearly was 666 talents, not including the revenues from merchants and traders and from all the Arabian kings and the governors of the territories.[22]

That is, Solomon 666 talents of gold each year in addition to the tolls levied by the customs officers, the profits on foreign trade, and the tribute of the kings of Arabia and the regional governors.

C. Access to Services

Along with the standard-of-living increases inherent in raising local employment, the presence of many business types can raise the standard-of-living further by providing a wider range of services and amenities in the local area.

Adding a movie theater to a small town, for example, can add an entertainment option to local residents while bringing in money from outlying communities.

D. Community-Focused Political Advantages

Businesses with strong ties to a local community can lend a hand in community-focused political actions. Businesses can help to fund and organize campaigns for lobbying, letter-writing and other political activities to influence legislators on issues that affect the local community.

A local business can help to convince a presidential candidate to hold a campaign speech in the town, for example, by making sizable campaign contributions.

---

[22] 1Kings 10:14-15

E. Cultivating Loyal Customers

Businesses with a local focus have the advantage of cultivating a loyal customer base, especially when their services are not threatened by big-box chain stores in the area.

While this may not influence company growth, it ensures a certain level of financial sustainability, and helps to ensure the company maintains a positive reputation in at least one region. It may also help small businesses get through tougher economic times, at least temporarily.

Tips for Starting a Christian Business

Each of us is born with unique God-given gifts and talents. Our gifts are expressed through hobbies, how we spend our free time and our choice of vocation.

What happens when you are called to use your strengths and talents to start your own business? How do you continue to honor the Lord along the rocky road of business ownership?

Before you make the decision to start a particular business, you must believe that there is value in that specific business, and that there is a need for the goods or services to be provided.

Starting a business is a massive challenge — the financial risks involved and vast amounts of time and dedication needed — requires a sizable leap of faith.

Starting a business requires faith and vision because it is faith, along with vision, that propels the entrepreneurs among us to forge ahead when others hold back. This makes taking the leap an important first step for success as a Christian entrepreneur.

- **Start a Business With Christian Ethics**

While all businesses are different, the Christian entrepreneur should keep in mind a few universal principles. Following these steps can help you balance your desire for professional success with your commitment to glorify the Lord in everything you do.

- **Remember From Whom All Blessings Flow**

Establishing and running a business requires confidence, and, some would argue, the self-assurance entrepreneurs need can turn into arrogance and self-reliance.

Lean on scripture to stay grounded. A reminder to remain modest is stated in Deuteronomy 8:18:

"But remember the Lord your God, for it is He who gives you the ability to produce wealth, and so confirms His covenant, which He swore to your ancestors, as it is today."

- **Honor God With Hard Work**

God calls on His people to work hard and not squander the talents and strengths He provided. All the noble men and women of the Bible were hardworking — in fact, many were working when they were called by God.

Again and again throughout scripture, God calls busy people. Romans 12:11 states:

"Do not be lazy but always work hard. Work for the Lord with a heart full of love for Him."

You must not be slothful for good stewardship and a desire to work heartily are celebrated.

- **Be Honest, Be Ethical.**

The right way to solve a customer's problem may not always be the most profitable for the business owner; when honoring God through our business remains our central motivation rather than profit, we will never turn away from our biblical work ethics. Mark 8:36 says:

"For what does it profit a man to gain the whole world and forfeit his soul?"

- **Give Thanks and Give Back**

Starting a business is not for the weak at heart. When hard work pays off and success is realized, it is all too easy to forget who gave the success and also forget to thank him for providing the blessings of courage and perseverance.

Remember to give thanks and honor to the Lord. For Christian entrepreneurs, giving back to God shows both your gratitude for and acknowledgment of His gifts, and also demonstrates your continued faith that the Lord will continue to provide and lead.

Proverbs 3: 9-10 says: *"Honor the Lord with your possessions and with the first produce of your entire harvest, then your barns will be completely filled, and your vats will overflow with new wine."*

- **Keep Praying**

Reaching a triumphant milestone like achieving your first profitable year, or serving your 100th customer, should not make your conversations with God to stop.

You must keep the lines of communication with God open at all times. Continue to be grateful, keep asking for guidance and always listen. God gives the best advice.

- **Succeed as a Christian Entrepreneur**

While succeeding as a Christian business owner requires a commitment to core Christian principles, it also takes business acumen.

A good way to develop both of these competencies is by enrolling for a business mentoring program. This will greatly help you and sharpen your business skill and help you to avoid the pitfalls that ruined the businesses of many.

- **Do not consume your first profit**

If your business must succeed in your business, then you must respect this commandment: **"Do not consume your first profit."** Can you use it to settle some personal problems? No! Recycle it.

Aliko Dangote: A contemporary example

Aliko Dangote GCON was born 10th of April 1957 in Kano, Kano State into a wealthy Hausa family. Dangote's mother, Mariya Sanusi Dantata, was the daughter of businessman Sanusi Dantata. Aliko Dangote's father, Mohammed Dangote, was a business associate of Sanusi Dantata. Through his mother, Dangote is the great-grandson of Alhassan Dantata, the richest West African at the time of his death in 1955.

He is a Nigerian business magnate who is the founder, chairman, and CEO of the Dangote Group, the largest industrial conglomerate in West Africa. According to Bloomberg Billionaires Index, Dangote's net worth is estimated at US$18.7 billion as of January 2023, making him the richest person in Africa and richest black person in the world.

Dangote was educated at the Sheikh Ali Kumasi Madrasa, followed by Capital High School, Kano. In 1978, he graduated from the Government College, Birnin Kudu. He received a bachelor's degree in business studies and administration from Al-Azhar University, Cairo.

He started the Dangote Group as a small trading firm in 1977, the same year he relocated to Lagos to expand the company. Dangote received a ₦500,000 loan from his uncle to begin trading in commodities including bagged cement as well as agricultural goods like rice and sugar.

In the 1990s, he approached the Central Bank of Nigeria with the idea that it would be cheaper for the bank to allow his transport company to manage their fleet of staff buses, a proposal that was also approved.

Today, the Dangote Group is one of the largest conglomerates in Africa, with international operations in Benin, Ghana, Zambia and Togo. The Dangote Group has moved from being a trading company to be the largest industrial group in Nigeria, encompassing divisions like Dangote Sugar Refinery, Dangote Cement, and Dangote Flour.

Dangote Group dominates the sugar market in Nigeria, with its refinery business is the main supplier (70 percent of the market) to the country's soft drink companies, breweries and confectioners. The company employs more than 11,000 people in West Africa.

In July 2012, Dangote approached the Nigerian Ports Authority to lease an abandoned piece of land at the Apapa Port, which was approved. He later built facilities for his sugar company there. It is the largest refinery in Africa and the third largest in the world, producing 800,000 tons of sugar annually.

The Dangote Group owns salt factories and flour mills and is a major importer of rice, fish, pasta, cement, and fertilizer. The company exports cotton, cashew nuts, cocoa, sesame seeds, and ginger to several countries. Additionally, it has major investments in real estate, banking, transport, textiles, oil, and gas.

In February 2022, Dangote announced the completion of Peugeot assembling facility in Nigeria following his partnership with Stellantis Group, the parent company of Peugeot, the Kano and Kaduna state government. The new automobile company, Dangote Peugeot Automobiles Nigeria Limited (DPAN) factory which is based in Kaduna commenced operations with the roll-out of Peugeot 301, Peugeot 5008, 3008, 508 and Land Trek."

Business made Dangote the Nigeria's first billionaire in 2007. Even Jesus sometimes calls us to learn wisdom from the sons of this age. Dangote started small! You may claim he was born into a wealthy family and that is why he could soar high but that is not true at all.

I use to know that most children from wealthy family are lazy dudes. They hide under the guise of their parents' wealth to refuse to engage themselves productively. Check around, how many children from wealthy families know the wisdom of hustling for loans to build their own wealth?

SECTION D
PARALLEL PASSAGES

5

Parallel Passages

Out of the 66 books of the entire Bible, the first 37 of the books are classified as the Old Testament (OT) while the last 29 books are classified as the New Testament (NT).

The 29 books of the NT are further classified as Gospels, Epistles and Apocalypse. The first four books of the NT are the Gospels. The books Romans, 1 & 2 Corinthians, Galatians, Ephesians, Philippians, Colossians, Titus, Philemon, and the remaining letters of Saint Paul are the epistles while the book of Revelation is the apocalypse.

A Gospel is a book of the Bible belonging to a set of four, Matthew, Mark, Luke, and John, that tell the story of the life of Jesus Christ.

From the 4 Gospels, three of them are regarded as "Synoptic Gospels." Synoptic Gospels are the gospels of Matthew, Mark, and Luke that tell the story of Jesus Christ's life and ministry from a similar point of view and are similar in structure.

In other words, the Gospels (Matthew, Mark and Luke) share some level of similarity. They are actually different books all about Jesus Christ but they are much similar in content even though there are a few variations here and there.

Note that I do not mean that every and any story found in Matthew is found in Mark and Luke. Some stories are peculiar to certain Gospels; however, these three books carry similar accounts. The Gospel of John is much more different in its content and structure from the three synoptic.

A good example of the similarity in contents of the synoptic Gospels is the 'Parable of the ten *minas*/servants' and the 'Parable of the three talents/servants'.

The parable of the three *talents* in Matthew 25 is like that of the ten *minas* found in the holy pages of Luke. The parable of the talents is the third in the series of three parables by which Matthew illustrates certain aspects of the coming of the Son of Man.

In the first parable found in 24:45-51, he warned against the danger of becoming so engrossed with the present that one fails to take into consideration the inevitability of the future. He warned against thinking that the master will take a very long period of time before he returns.

Then, in the second of the three parables found in 25:1-13, he warned against a future expectation that did not deal adequately with the present. It is a warning against a kind of thinking of the future return of the master without making adequate preparation in the present time.

Now, in this final one of the series found in 25:14-30, Matthew illustrates how the present must be lived in light of the future. How servants of the master must live while expecting the return of their master.

The theme of a long lapse of time is common to all three parables (24:48; 25:5; 25:19) and each of those parables seems to say that the master will not come just immediately, however, it must be known that he will not also take so long to return.

Let us take a look at the parable of the talents of Matthew 25,

14"Again, the Kingdom of Heaven can be illustrated by the story of a man going on a long trip. He called together his servants and entrusted his money to them while he was gone. 15He gave five bags of silver (**five talents**) *to one, two bags of silver* (**two talents**) *to another, and one bag of silver* (**one talent**) *to the last— dividing it in proportion to their abilities. He then left on his trip. 16"The servant who received the five bags of silver* (**five talents**) *began to invest the money and earned five more.*

17The servant with two bags of silver(**two talents**) *also went to work and earned two more* (**one talent**). *18But the*

servant who received the one bag of silver (**one talent**) dug a hole in the ground and hid the master's money. ¹⁹"After a long time their master returned from his trip and called them to give an account of how they had used his money.

²⁰The servant to whom he had entrusted the five bags of silver came forward with five more and said, 'Master, you gave me five bags of silver to invest, and I have earned five more.' ²¹"The master was full of praise. 'Well done, my good and faithful servant. You have been faithful in handling this small amount, so now I will give you many more responsibilities. Let's celebrate together!' ²²"The servant who had received the two bags of silver came forward and said, 'Master, you gave me two bags of silver to invest, and I have earned two more.'

²³"The master said, 'Well done, my good and faithful servant. You have been faithful in handling this small amount, so now I will give you many more responsibilities. Let's celebrate together!' ²⁴"Then the servant with the one bag of silver came and said, 'Master, I knew you were a harsh man, harvesting crops you didn't plant and gathering crops you didn't cultivate. ²⁵I was

afraid I would lose your money, so I hid it in the earth. Look, here is your money back.'

26"But the master replied, 'You wicked and lazy servant! If you knew I harvested crops I didn't plant and gathered crops I didn't cultivate, 27why didn't you deposit my money in the bank? At least I could have gotten some interest on it.' 28"Then he ordered, 'Take the money from this servant, and give it to the one with the ten bags of silver.

29To those who use well what they are given, even more will be given, and they will have an abundance. But from those who do nothing, even what little they have will be taken away. 30Now throw this useless servant into outer darkness, where there will be weeping and gnashing of teeth.'23

This parable of the *talents* holds some level of similarity to the parable of the *minas*. As I listen to several messages on the parable of the *minas* or the *talents* by preachers in and outside ECWA, I often discover that the preachers do not make a distinction between the two parables.

They zigzag in between the two parables and blend the two consciously and unconsciously. I am not against that but I am

---

23 *Matthew 25(NLT)*

simply trying to point to you how even modern day preachers agree that the two parables are similar.

Despite the similarity between the two parables, some key differences stand out. Go through the few differences between the two parables before we go ahead to see their similarity.

Differences between the parable of the minas and the parable of the talents

Matthean Rendering	Lukan Rendering
Matthew presents the parable as a parable of *talents*	Luke presents the parable as a parable of *minas*
Matthew did not specify the purpose of the master's journey.	Luke stated the purpose of the master's journey. To go and be crowned king.
Matthew did not specify the number of servants that the master called. Matthew only puts it that 3 servants were given talents	The Lukan account specified the number of servants called. 10 servants were called and given the *minas*.
Matthew specified that distribution of resources to the servants was done in proportion to their individual abilities.	Luke did not
Matthew puts it that the amount of talent each of them received varies (5:2:1).	Luke puts it that the servants all received equal amount of *minas*.
The "Occupy till I come" instruction is not in Matthew.	Luke's presentation of the parable spells that the servants

The Matthean rendering left the disciples clueless and so they could argue with the master for not telling them what to do with the money.	were not left clueless. They were told what to do with the money. To them the master gave this charge: "Occupy till I come."
The Matthean rendering of this parable did spells that the faithful servants were promoted and given more responsibility without stating what the responsibility was.	Lukan account of the parable indicates the type of new and bigger responsibilities given to the servants. From petty traders to rulers/governors of cities. This is to show that the "occupy till I come" instruction was to test the individual capacity of each servant. There are ways God tests us with little things and we do not even know. Sometimes we pass and sometimes we fail the tests. Our promotion and uplifting in life depends on how we treat his little instruction to us. Who would have known that he made these servants to become traders to prepare them for governorship positions? Do not belittle whatever God is asking you to do now for it is just a test that will determine whether or not you

	will be given much more responsibility and position.
	Life abounds with story of many servants of the master who were petty traders before God raised them into the current seat of power they now occupy.
	Some of them sold sachet water, some bought and sold grains, some sold second new clothing, etc. When God is putting them through that process, we never will know that the governorship of cities (states), of ministries or of corporations is what he is preparing them for.
	This is because a servant who must become a city governor must be well-disciplined. Governorship comes with authority, fame and money.
	A governor or a ruler of a city is the eye of the government in that place. He/she collects the revenues (taxes, tolls levied by the customs officers, the profits on foreign trade, and the tributes to the king) for the king who rules the entire empire.

The enemies of the master who sent a delegation against the master's rule are not mentioned in Matthean account of the parable.	The Lukan account of the parable did mentioned that the king had enemies and these enemies sent a delegation with a petition to register their unwillingness to submit to his ruler-ship.

The principal difference is, that the *minas* given to each servant seems to point out the gift of the gospel, which is the same to all who hear it; but the *talents*, distributed more or less, seem to mean that God gives different capacities and advantages to men, by which this one gift of the gospel may be differently improved.

However, whatever are the differences in the parables, it is needful to learn from the parables that the master furnishes his servants with gifts needful for their business; and he expects service from those to whom he gives power.

Again it is worthy of note that the master has given something to each of his servants (1Corinthians. 12:7; 1Peter 4:10). Our future position in His kingdom depends upon our present use of His grace—and that, having received His grace, we are to put it to diligent use and 'do business till He comes.'

Talents

I will be discussing the concept of *talents* in this chapter as we proceed in our study of what Jesus wants us to know from the parable of the *minas* and that of the *talents*. On most occasions, Jesus often packages spiritual truths and lessons of faith into short, relatable narratives known as parables.

These stories were his way of explaining the attributes of God and instructions for godly living in accessible human terms. And even though Jesus also used sermons to communicate, his use of story holds a special place in his ministry and teaching style.

From the parable of the *talents*, Jesus talked about a master who gave *talents* to his servants. To one servant, the master gives five *talents*, to a second servant he gives two *talents*, and to a third servant he gives one talent (Matthew 25:14-15).

My interest in this chapter is to discuss what a talent is in its literal and applied sense.

A *talent*, in this parable, refers to a unit of measurement, often used to weigh out silver or gold. The Greek word used for talent is τάλαντα; it is a Greek coin with value of 50006000 denarii. A denarius (δηνάριον, ου) was a Roman silver coin equivalent to the day's wage of a common laborer.[24]

A talent as a measure of weight varies in size from 28 to 36 kilograms, or 60 to 80 sixteen-ounce pounds, and was equivalent to 3,000 Hebrew shekels;

But as a large unit of money, it varies in value with the metal involved, whether gold, silver, or copper. The talent the master gave to his servants was made of gold thus, it was of high value. To put it in other words, it was really big money with high purchasing power.

A talent was a Greek monetary unit with a value which fluctuated; depending upon the particular monetary system which prevailed at a particular period of time (a silver talent was worth approximately six thousand denarii with gold *talents* worth at least thirty times that much).

According to the Complete Word Study Dictionary: New Testament, in the New Testament a talent indicates a large sum of money and the Bible Exposition Commentary: New Testament says that "this sum was maybe even as much as a million dollars in today's currency. No wonder the master was

---

[24] A Concise Greek-English Dictionary of the New Testament.

so upset with the servant who buried his one talent in the ground!"

However, the meaning of talent in and from the parable is different from the modern concept of a "talent" as a gift or natural ability. In the parable, the master entrusted his servants with a measure of his wealth, proportionate to each of their abilities (Matthew 25:15) but in our contemporary use, the word talent is not understood or used as a monetary unit.

• In Interpreting the Parables, Craig Blomberg identifies the *talents* as a portion of God's resources.

• I.H. Jones suggests we should consider *talents* as whatever endowment a Christian may have received.

• Brad H. Young includes everything that a person has, whether goods or abilities.

• John B. Carpenter gives a more open interpretation in his article, "The Parable of the *Talents* in Missionary Perspective." "Parables are about principles, and this parable is about faithfulness of endeavor." He goes on to say that the money was used as an example of everything with which we have been endowed by God and that we cannot identify the *talents* more specifically.

• R.T. France's commentary on Matthew argues that *talents* refer to "the specific privileges and opportunities of the kingdom of heaven...to be faithfully exploited before the master returns."

While D.A. Carson agrees that we cannot pin down the precise definition of talent. He said, "Attempts to identify the *talents* with spiritual gifts, the law, natural endowments, the gospel, or whatever else, leads to a narrowing of the parable with which Jesus would have been uncomfortable. Perhaps he chose the *talent* or *mina* symbolism because of its capacity for varied application.

In the most general sense, we can conclude that the *talents* are the tools God gives us to carry out the cultural mandate. In this context, we can be assured that whatever the Lord gives us now he will ask us about later, expecting us to diligently work with these resources for the furtherance of his kingdom.

Bearing all of these in mind, it becomes clear to us that there is no single meaning to the word talent. Many meanings can be implied depending on the spiritual lesson the Lord desires us to learn from the parable.

I want you to follow me as I discuss about the word 'talent' from a point of view that regards the *talents* of the parable as God given endowments.

Remember that the parable is just a story with a hidden meaning. And so, the talent (money) that the master gave to his servant represents whatever God has giving us – his followers.

There are many things that God has giving to humanity (Life, Rain, Food, Clothing, etc.) but I want to talk about something special and specific that God has giving humanity which is ABILITY. I want to talk about abilities as a connotative (implied additional) meaning of the *talents* in the parable.

Abilities are enablement given to man by God. As human beings, we have shaped the world to the current stage because of certain abilities we possess which were given to us by God or otherwise. It is God's desire for us to trade, invest, engage, do business and make profit with all the abilities that we received from him.

Please note that my reference to the *talent* as abilities we received from God is not the precise meaning of the talent in the parable. I am only discussing it as implied additional meaning of the *talents* in the parable to broaden and deepen our understanding of the parable of the *talents*.

Among theologians, John Calvin has shaped much of our understanding of the word *talent*. However, many contemporary theologians have offered alternative views. It is a fascinating discussion.

John Calvin's Interpretation of the Word "Talent"
According to Paul Marshall in his book A Kind of Life Imposed on Man: Vocation and Social Order from Tyndale to Locke, Calvin helped shape the modern meaning of the word

talent by his revolutionary change in the interpretation of the parable of the *talents*.

He defined the *talents* as gifts from God in the form of a person's calling or natural ability. Calvin made it clear that the use of our *talents* is not restricted to the church or to its pious duties. It encompasses the whole of creation.

Marshall reports that Calvin challenged believers "to work, to perform, to develop, to progress, to change, to choose, to be active, and to overcome until the day of their death or the return of their Lord."

Many biblical scholars have expanded on Calvin's definition of the word *talent* to mean abilities, while also expressing caution to avoid reading current meanings of the word back into the parable.

Classification of Abilities

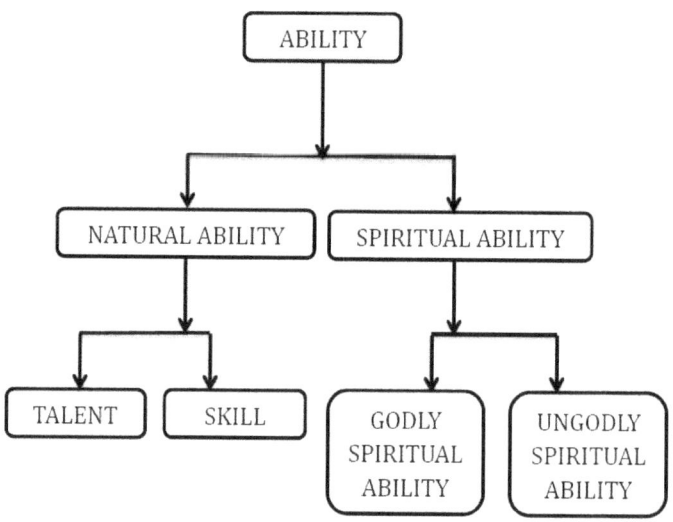

God has given us abilities which like the *talents* vary from one person to another. These abilities are grouped as 'Natural abilities' and 'Spiritual abilities'.

The Natural abilities are further classified based on how they are acquired as 'Talent' and 'Skill' while the Spiritual abilities are also classified into two base on their sources.

The spiritual world/realm does not consist only of God and his holy angels. The devil and demons also constitute what is referred to as the spiritual world/realm. It is needful to understand that both worlds give abilities to humans.

Scripture abounds with individuals who displayed certain spiritual abilities that were given to them by God and many individuals who also displayed certain spiritual abilities that were not given to them by God but from the devil. We shall see examples of such later.

The spiritual abilities distributed by the Holy Spirit of God are 'Godly Spiritual Abilities'; these are also known as 'Spiritual Gifts' but the spiritual abilities distributed by evil spirits are 'Ungodly Spiritual Abilities.

A. Natural Abilities
These are abilities that are natural. One's faith allegiance does not qualify or disqualify him/her from possessing them. A natural ability speaks of one's capacity, capability, potential, potentiality, power, faculty, aptness, facility, propensity, wherewithal, means or preparedness that comes naturally to him. It is not from his/her association with any spirit.

These types of abilities are categorized into two: Talents and Skills.

a. Talent

In the contemporary, a talent refers to a natural ability: an unusual and exceptional natural ability to do something well, especially in artistic areas that can be developed by training.

It is synonymous to a gift, aptitude, flair, bent, knack, genius, etc. but some key differences exist in their meanings.

* In a Christian sense, a *gift* is also an ability possessed only by a believer. This kind of gift is distributed by the Holy Spirit. I shall dwell more on this concept shortly.

* An *aptitude* is a natural tendency to do something well, especially one that can be further developed.

* A *flair* is also a natural ability to do something well, especially creative or artistic ability.

* *Bent* is a strong natural inclination or liking for something. Technical schools were for students who had a practical bent.

* *Knack* refers to a particular skill, especially one that might be innate or intuitive and therefore difficult to teach.

* *Genius* is an exceptional intellectual or creative ability.

A talent is much the same with all the above except a Gift. A talent is the natural ability to do something better than most people. It is often confused with skill but the two are different. We can self-acquire skills but we cannot self-acquire talents because we just open our eyes and discover that we have this or that talent.

We may see someone with a talent to play football very well and decide to learn how to do that even though we are not talented for that. If we learn and can do that which he/she does when we do not have the talent for that, it is called a Skill. Meaning skills can be self-acquired and self-improved but talent cannot be self-acquired and self-improved.

An individual who has a talent was born with it. He or she cannot explain when and how he/she is able to do the thing he/she is talented to do. A talent is the information written in genes when we are born. That information never changes in our lifetime. It can only be inherited by our children.

Talent is a greater potential for doing something. But talent is not enough. To get good results we need also practice. Even the greatest talent without practice will not give good skill.

But on the other hand, even years of practice without talent will not give good results either. If somebody has no talent for music but learns to play piano several hours a day for two years, they will achieve some skill but never become a great musician.

- *Talents Are Inherited*

Talents are those abilities inherited from one's parents and nurtured in the context of one's family. We all know people who are talented and come from a long line of family members who share the same talent.

(Consider, for example, the Jahslave's family in Adunu. All his four children – both males and females are talented musicians from childhood. The children inherited that talent from their father. It is just that: "natural"!)

Talents can be attributed to the natural genetic material existing within all of us, passed down from generation to generation.

- *Talents Are Possessed by the Believer and Unbeliever*

Everyone, whether they are a believer or a non-believer, has some sort of talent, but only believers have spiritual gifts.

Talents are natural abilities that anyone can possess irrespective of his or her allegiance to God. This is one of the places where talents differ from Godly Spiritual Abilities.

For example, not all the talented people on earth are Christians. There are a lot of talented individuals in the sport and music industry, security and information agencies, architects, automobile designers and the movie industry who are not believers, yet, they are talented. Once they are in action, you cannot deny that their performance is superb.

The only difference is that the believer can possess both natural and godly spiritual abilities, while the non-believer cannot. At best, the non-believer can possess both natural and ungodly spiritual ability but the godly spiritual ability (gifts) is the sole heritage for and only of the believer.

b. Skills

A Skill is an ability to do something well, usually gained through training or experience. An individual who is not talented genetically for music can decide to learn to do music by constant training and practice.

He/she can gain a music skill not because he/she inherited it from his/her parent. It is just a skill but talent is not gotten through training and experience. Training and practice only improves ones' talent.

Skill is often confused with Talent but the two are different. We can self-acquire skills but we cannot self-acquire talents because we just open our eyes and discover that we have this or that talent.

But we may see someone with a talent to play football very well and decide to learn how to do that even though we are not talented for that. If we learn and can do that which he/she does when we do not have the talent for that, it is called a Skill. Meaning skills can be self-developed and self-improved but talent cannot be self-developed but can be self-improved.

Talent Killers

There are four things that kill highly talented people: yea, even five that bury them:

1. Pride after success

This often starts when a person becomes aware of his or her talents. He sees that he can do certain things in ways people around him cannot readily do, and not necessarily because of his preparation.

Also, when he begins to get recognition for the things he is doing right, the tendency is for him to bask in that euphoria for so long that he forgets the place of hard work.

So, he stops learning. Stops following rules and stops growing. The end product is just the freezing of his talent or a complete waste of it in a maze of inconsistencies.

Pride is often considered the biggest killer of success, that is partly true. I say "partly" because pride always precedes destruction, but some of the points listed below can be as dangerous if not more.

Pride can also breed jealousy and envy. Now, those are deadly combinations.

2. Shame after failure

This is a major killer of talented individuals. Because of several successes that they have recorded, talented people often do not understand what it means to fail. So, when faced with failure, they withdraw into their shells to bemoan their state.

Some go even farther by disbelieving themselves and what they are capable of accomplishing. So, you will hear things like "I don't think I'm talented at all. I don't have what it takes to do this. If I were talented, I wouldn't have failed." Others end up depressed and even become unable to try again.

Unfortunately, what they do not realize is that even the most successful people in life failed several times and still fail. That no matter how talented you are, life will present a stark reality to you: *"you can only get as far as here with your talent. To go beyond this point, you have to pay some dues."*

It is now left for the talented person to pick himself up, believe in what he's got and go back to learn why he failed, improve on it and bounce back. It is easier said than done for some of them.

3. Procrastination instead of being proactive

Yes! This point is so crucial. This is a great waster of talents. If you are talented, one thing you must recognize is that your talents are NEVER enough; they are not sufficient on their own to catapult you to the enviable height of your dreams.

If you played for the amateur club on your street and competed with the next street, chances are that you will win easily because you do not follow strict rules and maybe the other players are not as skillful as you are on the ball. But when you begin to compete on the state or national level, you will soon discover that there are many talented and skilled players everywhere, who have mastered the art of dribbling and defense too.

So, added to talent is hard work, consistent training and a winning mindset. But some very talented people procrastinate a lot. They are never available to work on their talents and improve on their weaknesses.

Procrastination is like not adhering to therapy because you feel that the disease is not worth the stress. Well, you will take that therapy later but maybe at a higher dosage and for a longer period of time because in the meantime the disease condition has worsened. Take the pains now to train yourself; else your talents will not amount to much.

4. Doubt (Fear) instead of trying

This could be a resultant effect of point 2 above, that is, the feeling of shame after a failure could cause fear. But fear can also develop in the absence of failure. However it develops, when fear dominates, talent shrinks and its carrier becomes paralyzed.

These includes: The Fear of not being good enough, Fear of what people will say, Fear of performing at high levels, The

Fear of failure, Fear of managing success and Fear that people will discover that I am not good enough after all.

These and many other fears make several talented people waste their talents in local leagues when they should be plying their trade internationally.

It was fear that made that one with one talent to bury it for fear that if he tries to trade with the money, he will fail. Fear destroys!

5. *Thinking of and living for what other people think*

This is a brutal killer. It not only kills, but it also buries the individual. Many highly talented people are wasting away because of what they think other people think about them. And sometimes, people are not even thinking about those things they think that they are thinking.

Others believe all the negative opinions and views of their friends, colleagues and people they trust that they are simply paralyzed.

Then, there is a category of people who live to please others by not expressing their talents. They feel that being average is synonymous with humility or that expressing their talents would discomfort those around them. So, they prefer to remain dormant until further notice. Well, they further notice never arrives.

Hiding your talent is as good as hiding a lit candle under the basket or bed. This will be great folly. The instructions Jesus left for us is this:

> *Ye are the light of the world. A city that is set on an hill cannot be hid. Neither do men light a candle, and put it under a bushel, but on a candlestick; and it giveth light unto all that are in the house. Let your light so shine before men, that they may see your good works, and glorify your Father which is in heaven.*[25]

This list is not the exhaustive list of things that kill talents but happy are those that overcome these, for they shall manifest their talents to the fullest. Let men so feel the impact of your talent so that they can glorify your father in heaven.

Developing our talents

You have a responsibility to develop the talents you have been given. Sometimes you think you do not have many talents or that other people have been blessed with more abilities than you possess.

Sometimes you do not use your talents because you are afraid that you might fail or be criticized by others. But you must not

---

[25] Matthew 5:14-16

hide your talents. You should use them. Then others can see your good works and glorify your Heavenly Father (see Matthew 5:16).

Talents and gifts are all tools and avenues given to you by God to serve mankind in solving certain problems. And you are going to be rewarded by life from the problems you solve. If you do not use your gift and horn them to be very sharp, you will achieve very little.

Payment is a reward given in return for a problem solved. There are different kind of talents and abilities on earth because their different kind of problems on earth. Abilities (talents and gifts) are resources given to us by God to enable us solve or manage some problems.

It is when you discover your talent and use it to solve problems that men are obliged to pay you. Do not expect money when you are not solving any problem on earth. Even God will not give you open doors when there is no need to be met with it. Your reward in life is determined by how you use the abilities God gives you.

For that reason, you must pay the price necessary to develop/horn your gift.

There are certain things you must do to develop our talents.

i.   First, you must discover your talents. You can do this by evaluating yourself to find your strengths and abilities. Your family and friends can help you do this.

You should also ask your Heavenly Father to help you learn about your talents.

ii. Second, you must be willing to spend the time and effort to develop the talent you are seeking.

iii. Third, you must have faith that your Heavenly Father will help you, and you must have faith in yourself.

iv. Fourth, you must learn the skills necessary for you to develop your talents. You might do this by taking a class, asking a friend to teach you, or reading a book.

If you are talented with business acumen, you may want to listen to the teachings and read books of great entrepreneurs like Robert Kiyosaki, Elon Musk, etc.

I know of a friend (Ishaya Abel) who is blessed with great business talents and he knew this. When my wife and I noticed that too, we tried to persuade him to attend online classes of Kiyosaki, read business books, so that he can develop this gift, I pray he do that someday.

As I write this book, he is excelling in this talent but he would have done more exploits with this talent if he devotes his time to develop this talent.

v.   Fifth, you must practice using your talent. Every talent takes effort and work to develop. The mastery of a talent must be earned.

vi.   Sixth, you must share your talent with others. It is by using your talents that they grow (see Matthew 25:29). President Joseph F. Smith said, "Every son and every daughter of God has received some talent, and each will be held to strict account for the use or misuse to which it is put" (Gospel Doctrine, 5th ed. [1939], 370).

A talent is one kind of stewardship (responsibility in the kingdom of God). The parable of the talents tells us that when you serve well in your stewardship, you will be given greater responsibilities. If you do not serve well, your stewardship will eventually be taken from you. (See Matthew 25:14–30.)

By developing and using your talents for other people, you perform good works and the Lord will be pleased.

All of these steps are easier if you pray and seek the Lord's help. He wants you to develop your talents, and He will help you.

We all have weaknesses because we are mortal and fallen. Yet, we can develop our talents in spite of our weaknesses. With the Lord's help, our weakness and fallen nature can be overcome.

Some great athletes have had to overcome handicaps before they have succeeded in developing their talents. The great footballer Lionel Messi is such an example. He had great soccer talent but suffered a disease of duarfism in his childhood before the club Barcelona picked him up and sponsored his treatment. Lionel Messi rose to become the GOAT (Greatest Of All Time) of the game of soccer.

"That which we persist in doing becomes easier for us to do; not that the nature of the thing is changed, but that our power to do is increased" (in Teachings of Presidents of the Church: Heber J. Grant [2002], 35).

B. Spiritual Abilities

Aside the abilities that are natural, there are certain abilities that are beyond the natural. Such abilities are supernatural. They may not be acquired at birth and such abilities may just come to a person in the middle of the road.

The individual may be born without a particular ability and all of a sudden, he/she possess the ability without having learned it from anyone. This kind ability just shows up overnight. This was the type of ability that manifested in Acts 2 on the day of Pentecost when the disciples were in the upper room.

To think that all spiritual abilities are from God is product of a narrow understanding. An individual who has an ability to communicate with spirits of the dead and tell the destiny of another person has a spiritual ability because such ability is not natural. However, such ability is not of God and so, it is necessary to classify spiritual abilities into two: ungodly spiritual ability and godly spiritual ability.

1. Ungodly Spiritual Ability

I mentioned earlier to you that it is not all unnatural abilities that come from God. Because we confirm from the Holy Scriptures that there are some people that possess some spiritual abilities that do not belong to God.

I am never trying to equate God with the devil. No, far from that! My point is that, devil also gives "Spiritual Abilities" to mankind. You will find an individual with a certain ability that is not a talent or a skill.

If such ability is not naturally gotten, and is not learnt naturally then it is an ungodly spiritual ability. I have explained to you what is a talent and examples of talents. If you understand that, then I am not referring to talents.

I am talking about supernatural abilities that did not come from God but from the evil world. Godly spiritual abilities can be referred to as "Spiritual Gifts" or simply as "Gifts" but this category of spiritual abilities cannot be called gifts because they are not given as a gift. This is because any gift worthy of its name is free but these ungodly spiritual abilities are not

138

freely given. Anyone who accepts them from the devil has a price to pay knowingly or unknowingly.

Biblical examples of individuals who showcased ungodly spiritual abilities include the following;

    a.   The slave girl who could predict the future (Acts 16:16)

> *A female slave had a spirit by which she predicted the future...She followed Paul and the rest of us, shouting, "These men are servants of the Most High God, who are telling you the way to be saved." She kept this up for many days. Finally Paul became so annoyed that he turned around and said to the spirit, "In the name of Jesus Christ I command you to come out of her!" At that moment the spirit left her.*

Fortune-telling, divining, psychic power, second sight, extrasensory perception, ESP, sixth sense, telepathy, prophecy, fortune telling, palm reading, astrology, soothsaying, augury are not natural abilities nor mal to a normal human being.

Such abilities are sourced from elsewhere but not from the Holy Spirit of God. Remember that it is only every good and perfect gift that comes from God.

b. Simon the Sorcerer (Acts 8:9-11)

Now for some time a man named Simon had practiced sorcery in the city and amazed all the people of Samaria. He boasted that he was someone great, and all the people, both high and low, gave him their attention and exclaimed, "This man is rightly called the Great Power of God." They followed him because he had amazed them for a long time with his sorcery.

Sorcery is witchcraft, wizardry, magic, black magic, enchantment, witchery, necromancy (literary), bewitchment and conjuring. And the precious Holy Spirit of my God cannot be a distributor of such evil abilities.

Even if a person is born with these kinds of abilities, they cannot be termed as natural talents because such abilities are spiritual in their sense.

No warning can be clearer than this:

[10]Let no one be found among you who sacrifices their son or daughter in the fire, who practices divination or sorcery, interprets omens, engages in witchcraft, [11]or

casts spells, or who is a medium or spiritist or who consults the dead. ¹²Anyone who does these things is detestable to the Lord; because of these same detestable practices the Lord your God will drive out those nations before you. ¹³You must be blameless before the Lord your God.

2. Godly Spiritual Ability

These kinds of abilities are referred to as "spiritual gifts" or simply "gifts" that are given to and can only be possessed by Christians. They are given and distributed by the Holy Spirit.

If you see any non-Christian operating with the type of abilities that will be discussed below, then it comes naturally to them as a talent or they secured it spiritually from the evil world.

Spiritual Gifts are Received

Spiritual gifts come directly from the Spirit of God; that is why they are called "gifts" in the first place! The "Spirit works all these things, distributing to each one individually just as He wills." Natural talents are imparted at our natural birth but spiritual gifts are given to us when we are born again.

Gifts Are Possessed by the Saved

Everyone, whether they are a believer or a non-believer, has some sort of talent, but only believers have spiritual gifts.

The Spirit of God resides in each and every believer, and "God has allotted to each Christian a measure of faith," and an ability transcending our natural talents. Because the Spirit of God is the source for spiritual gifts, we must not be surprised those who have God's Spirit residing in them (those who are saved), would have more than natural talents.

Aside the natural abilities we are born with, believers have gifts of the Spirit. These gifts are enablement given to each Christian to enable him/her fulfill his own task and assignment in the body of Christ.

    a. The word of wisdom
    b. The word of knowledge
    c. Faith (extraordinary trust and surrender)
    d. Gifts of healing
    e. The effecting of miracles
    f. Prophecy
    g. The distinguishing of spirits
    h. Tongues
    i. The interpretation of tongues
    j. Service
    k. Teaching
    l. Exhortation
    m. Giving
    n. Leadership
    o. Mercy
    p. Apostleship
    q. Evangelism
    r. Pastoral care

Some spiritual gifts (like j. k. m. n) sound a lot like natural abilities and you may know a Non-believer who is very talented in some of these areas without having been given a gift of the Spirit. Such ability in the life of the non-believer is just a talent and not a gift.

But there are other gifts on the list that is specific to the lives of believers. If any non-believer possesses them, he/she did not just inherit them from his parents. Such must have been acquired from the devil and his agents. If you see any non-believer with these believer specific gifts/abilities, then what is at work in him or her is just the counterfeit of the true gifts of God.

※ *Gifts Are Matured and Surprising*

If you are a talented leader and you then become a Christian and God decides to use you in some role of leadership, you just may find that your talent is greatly multiplied when God also gives you the spiritual gift of leadership.

You may then discover your leadership skills are above and beyond anything you were capable of doing prior to being saved. God has a tendency to surprise us in this way.

We can all develop our natural talents with hard work and perseverance; we practice and train and along the way we can achieve the expected results. Spiritual gifts, on the other hand, are increased as we mature in our relationship with God.

When we have been gifted by God to accomplish something, we should expect the unexpected. As we mature in our relationship with God, he will surprise us by gifting us beyond our natural talent.

✻ *Gifts Are Used to Serve God's Purposes*

The Bible clearly tells us that spiritual gifts are given to us for a specific reason. They are not given to us to serve our own selfish interests and desires, spiritual gifts have been given to us by God "for the common good" and to the glory of God; they are given to us so we can give them back to God as we serve His purpose of building the family of believers.

Spiritual gifts are given to us so all of us can perform "the work of service, to the building up of the body of Christ". That is why all of us are gifted in some way by God. We are not supposed to sit and watch the pastor do the work, we are supposed to get out and use the gifts God has given us.

There are three lists of spiritual gifts in the Bible (Rom 12, 1Co 12, and Eph 4:10). In my opinion, the most detailed is that reported by Paul to the Corinthians. That consists of the gifts of:

- *Message of Wisdom*: It is the ability the Holy Spirit gives a person to offer wise counsel based on the Word of God.
  The word of wisdom is a divine insight into people and situations that is not obvious to the average person. It is

a God-given wisdom that is combined with an understanding of what to do and how to do it.

- *Message of knowledge*: it is the ability that the Holy Spirit gives a person to have a special knowledge about a situation or someone.

  It is a revelatory knowledge, that is, it is knowledge that is revealed by God. It is not a kind of knowledge acquired through education or study. People with this gift can see a total stranger and know some details about him/her.

- *Ability to prophesy*: it does not necessarily consist in predicting a future situation, but rather in uttering a special message from the Holy Spirit.

  A person with this gift speaks by the special inspiration of God to communicate an immediate message to God's people.

- *Faith*: it does not refer to the habitual faith that every Christian should have in regard to salvation. But it is a supernatural ability given by the Holy Spirit to trust God fully in any situation.

  This kind of faith knows no impossibilities; it puts no limits to what god can do. This gift enables the person to trust God in difficult circumstances with a supernatural confidence.

- *Healing*: As the name itself says, it is the ability the Holy Spirit gives to someone to pray for cures. A believer with the gift of healing has the ability to let God's power flow through him to restore health apart from the use of natural methods. "Healing" means to make well.

- *Miraculous powers*: it is the gift that the Holy Spirit gives to someone to show supernatural situations.

  Through individuals with this gift, God performs powerful acts which are beyond the possibility of occurring naturally.

- *Distinguishing between spirits*: it is the discernment that the Holy Spirit gives to someone so that he knows when a message comes directly from God or from a deceiver. Such persons are able to evaluate people, doctrines, and situations as to whether they are of God or of Satan.

- *Variety of tongues*: refers to spiritual language. Which the Spirit gives us for our own edification.

- *Interpretation of tongues*: refers to the ability to understand what different languages mean. The only way to build up the church through prayer in tongues is if there is also an interpreter.

✹ *There is no individual who has all the gifts*

There is no individual who has all the gifts. God deliberately made it so, so that there will be core-dependency among believers. God do not want you to be all sufficient, he wants you to need others and so, it is a settled matter that no human has ever or will ever possess all the spiritual gifts needed for the edification of the Church.

It is possible to have more than one or two or even more gifts but it is impossible to have all the spiritual abilities. The church (all believers) as a body has many parts and each has its specific function and should be satisfied in using the tools given to it by God for the edification of the whole body.

No one part of the body is capable of executing all the functions of the body and so you alone cannot do all or have all the gifts. (1Corinthians 12:14)

The prophet Moses was a great leader, but he needed Aaron, his brother, to help as a spokesman (see Exodus 4:14–16). Some of us are leaders like Moses or good speakers like Aaron. Some of us can sing well or play an instrument. Others may be good in sports or able to work well with our hands but none of us can do all things needful of the church.

This mechanism was designed by God to help prevent believers from dabbling into pride. If God were to allow any believer to possess all the spiritual gifts, then he/she can do all things therefore becomes the almighty that is self-sufficient.

But God wants us to be unable to do certain things not to preserve his seat as God but so that you will value other believers who can do those things you cannot do.

It is important to also make it clear that there is no gift that is of less importance, but all gifts must be used for the glory of God. Every Spiritual ability/gifts you have has only one purpose, to glorify God

As believers, we must know the purpose of the gifts and talents that are given to us by God. These gifts that are entrusted to our hands are not toys neither are they possessions that we obtained by some merit or by being super–special Christians. They are tools delivered into our hands for helping in the work of the Kingdom of God.[26]

Difference Between Talents And Gifts

TALENTS	GIFTS
Talents are natural	Gifts are supernatural

---

[26] I Peter 4:10-11 [10]Each of you should use whatever gift you have received to serve others, as faithful stewards of God's grace in its various forms. [11]If anyone speaks, they should do so as one who speaks the very words of God. If anyone serves, they should do so with the strength God provides, so that in all things God may be praised through Jesus Christ. To him be the glory and the power for ever and ever. Amen.

Talents are inherited from one's parents, ultimately from Adam	Gifts are received from God
Talents are received at birth; they are natural endowments.	Gifts are received at the time of the new birth
Talents are possessed both by saved people and by unsaved people. There are many unsaved people who are very talented (musical ability, artistic ability, athletic ability, mathematical ability, etc.).	Gifts are possessed only by saved people, those who are members of the church which is His Body. An unsaved person might mimic a spiritual gift, but it is counterfeit and limited to self-activity (e.g.-a false prophet, a false teacher, etc.).
A man may be very talented as a TEACHER in the public school system or at a prestigious university. He may be recognized as an outstanding teacher by all of his co-workers. He may be very talented when it comes to communication skills and oratory. He may even win the "Teacher of the Year" Award.	This same man, upon believing on the Lord Jesus Christ, may not receive the gift of teaching. Spiritual gifts are determined by God not by any natural talents which a man may possess. If this same man should receive the gift of teaching it is above and beyond and distinct from any natural teaching talent which he had. It is something that he did not have prior to the new birth.

For full effectiveness talents need to be developed. A person who is naturally skilled musically must still learn to play an instrument, often demanding years of practice. Most professional athletes not only have natural talent but they have developed this talent through years of practice and hard work.	Gifts need to be exercised and this can only happen as the believer stays spiritually healthy and grows "in the grace and knowledge of the Lord Jesus Christ" (2 Peter 3:18). The proper exercise of spiritual gifts requires spiritual growth and maturity (Ephesians 4:13-16).
Talents possessed by believers ought to be surrendered and consecrated to the Lord and used for His honor and glory. Example: A skilled organist playing for a worship service "as unto the Lord."	Gifts are given by God for the outworking of God's LIFE as expressed by the Body of Christ. When the Body is healthy the LIFE of God is manifested and God is glorified (compare 1 Corinthians 14:24-25).

"There is a difference between natural talents and supernatural gifts. Talents come through the genes of natural inheritance; gifts directly by the Lord. Talent comes from the first Adam and, however attractive, is still a part of man's fallen nature. The gift is by the Holy Spirit, as it pleases Him" (Carlton Helgerson, *The Local Church*, pages 34-35).

Despite the major differences between gifts and talents, there is one similarity between the two and that is the fact that both are blessings from God, the Creator of all things. He gives these abilities to mankind so that he who possesses them can do at least something to benefit the world to the glory and honor of God.

Safeguarding Spiritual Gifts

From the parable of the talent, the servant who did not invest the talent given to him gave this as his reason:

> *'Master, I know you have high standards and hate careless ways, that you demand the best and make no allowances for error. I was afraid I might disappoint you, so I found a good hiding place and secured your money. Here it is, safe and sound down to the last cent.'*
>
> **MSG**

He failed to trade with the talent his master gave to him because of fear – fear of losing what he was given. He was afraid he might waste his master's money and so he found a good hiding place and secured the money. And when his master came to take account of what each of them did with the money, this servant answered saying, "Here it is, safe and sound down to the last cent."

I want you to note that this servant was not punished for lavishing his master's money. He did not waste the talent given to him, he saved the talent. He preserved and guarded the talent from loss. If I can explain his answer in other words, I would put it as this:

"Master, I protected your money from wastage. I did not allow anything to happen to your money."

Remember that we are discussing these talents as gifts. From the instructional manual on how to excel in ministry that apostle Paul sent to Timothy, we find this charge

"Timothy, guard what God has entrusted to you."
1Timothy 6 (NIV)

In this section, I intend to discuss about guarding the spiritual gifts that God has given us. From the verse above, it is clear that the gifts that God gives us need to be guarded. The gifts of God to us need to be protected and kept from harm.

There is an undying argument over what Paul meant when he said *"God's gifts and his call can never be withdrawn."* Romans 11:29 NLT. The two arguments over this verse are:

A. The gifts of God cannot be revoked or withdrawn once they are given. Irrespective of what or how the recipients of the gifts behave, spiritual gifts are permanent. A person can never lose his spiritual gifts. "God never takes back his gifts or revokes his choice."

B. Spiritual gifts are temporal; God can withdraw them from a person if he/she does not behave well. A person can lose his spiritual gifts. Romans 11:29 is not talking about spiritual gifts, it is talking about God's promise to the nation of Israel.

These are the two arguments concerning this verse. Many Christians have asked and are still asking this same question: *"Can a Christian lose his spiritual gift?"*

I do not want to enter into arguments but I do love to give you an answer to this question from the instruction Paul gave Timothy.

The word *"Guard"* means to protect somebody or something against danger or loss by being vigilant and taking defensive measures. It could also mean to prevent somebody or something from escaping.

I will use the first meaning to answer the question. There are certain things that can hurt our spiritual gifts. Our spiritual gifts are not indestructible; there are some things that harm godly spiritual gifts. I am not talking about whether or not God can take away our gifts.

There are certain things that are very dangerous and hazardous to godly spiritual gifts. Those are the kind of things that Paul warned Timothy to watch out for, to guard against them. Timothy had the gifts of God in him that he needed to Guard.

The same applies to you and I. There is need for you and I to guard the spiritual gifts that God has given us. If we do not do so, the gifts can be harmed or wasted. If the servant who guarded his talent was punished for not investing the talent, what will then be the hope of a servant who allowed his gifts to hurt?

It is your duty to safeguard and protect your spiritual gifts by the help of the Holy Spirit. The devil has set so many strategies in place that seek to keep you from making the best use of your spiritual gifts. But you must watch out against such.

How Do We Guard our Spiritual gifts?

* What are the foxes that ruin spiritual gifts?
* In what ways can we be vigilant against the foxes that ruin spiritual gifts?
* How can we take defensive measures against this foxes?

I shall only say what I see in scriptures. In the two volumes of ministerial instructions that Paul sent to Timothy, there are certain things Paul urged Timothy to shun, to avoid and to flee from. And I believe these were the things that Paul knew could harm the good deposit that God entrusted to Timothy.

If the gifts of God in us cannot be harmed by anything, then Paul will not suffer to urge Timothy to guard his own gifts.

Spiritual gifts are susceptible to harm and hazard and so, they must be jealously protected from the assault of the enemy.

Spiritual gifts are the driving forces that enable the Church to withstand the antics of Satan. We cannot succeed by natural strength alone and the devil knows that we need the divine and supernatural enablement that come by the working of spiritual gifts to succeed as Christians.

That is why he is out to make us err in the use of our gifts, to make our gifts lose their cutting edge, to prevent us from ever discovering them or to prevent us from developing and deploying our spiritual gifts.

Below is a list of some things that can exert some negative damage to our spiritual gifts and how we can guard our spiritual gifts against them:

i. *Avoid godless, foolish discussions with those who oppose you with their so-called knowledge. [21]Some people have wandered from the faith by following such foolishness.* **1Timothy 6 (NIV)**

ii. *[16]But shun profane and vain babblings: for they will increase unto more ungodliness. [17]And their word will eat as doth a canker: of whom is*

Hymenaeus and Philetus; [18]*Who concerning the truth have erred,*

2Timothy 2 (NKJV)

iii.　[7a]*Do not waste time arguing over godless ideas and old wives' tales.* [16]*Keep a close watch on how you live and on your teaching. Stay true to what is right for the sake of your own salvation and the salvation of those who hear you.* **1Timothy 4 (NLT)**

iv.　*Flee also youthful lusts: but follow righteousness, faith, charity, peace, with them that call on the Lord out of a pure heart.* [23]*But foolish and unlearned questions avoid, knowing that they do gender strives.*

2Timothy 2:22 (NKJV)

If a Christian did not take time to avoid the things we are warned to ignore here, he will shipwreck. He will depart from the faith, and go into error. Paul gave us example of two persons that incurred this kind of shipwreck, Hymenaeus and Philetus.

It is my desire for you to be vigilant and watch out for these cancerous lifestyles and acts that ruins our spiritual adventure. But remember that "*Master, I was afraid I might disappoint you, so I found a good hiding place and secured your money. Here it is, safe and sound down to the last cent"* is not enough.

As we guard our spiritual gifts, we need to develop and use them if not it is still vanity. We must guard and fan our spiritual gifts to flame.

Fanning/Developing Spiritual Gifts

Any true development comes at a price. Individuals who wish to develop, stir and fan their gifts must be willing to make the sacrifice necessary for their kind of gift.

Spiritual gifts are supernatural enablement that God distributes to his followers uniquely so that each of them can participate in the kingdom service.

A spiritual gift is something God has chosen specifically for you so that you can help with the advancement of the church on earth by serving and using your special ability.

These gifts are automatic divine enablements which equip us to serve beyond our natural strength. However, these gifts must be developed (fanned) before we can function at our best. It is possible to have a gift that is laying dormant waiting for when it will be developed for kingdom service.

For each gift, there are practicable things you can do to improve it. This development will make the gift to so shine before men. It will enable us to make the best use of the spiritual gift. While I hope to mention a few scriptural things you can do to develop your spiritual gift, I will please refer you to the section on how to develop talents discussed previously.

Paul did not leave his spiritual son in the dark concerning what and what he must do to fan his spiritual gift to flame:

i. *⁶And the special gift of ministry you received when I laid hands on you and prayed—keep that ablaze!*

The practice of laying hands on people was common in the early church for several functions, among which are: (1) healing (for example, Mark 8.23RSV); (2) bestowing a blessing (see, for example, Mark 10.16RSV); (3) making it possible for people to receive the Holy Spirit (for example, Acts 8.17RSV); and (4) setting people apart for certain functions (see, for example, Acts 13.3RSV).

This last function is in focus in the present context. In the history of the church, the laying on of hands has become an important part of the rite of ordination, that is, of setting apart certain people for specific church offices.

It is not altogether certain, however, whether in the present context the formal ordination of Timothy is meant or, less formally, his commissioning to a certain task.

This is complicated by the fact that, while various church offices are discussed in the letter, nowhere is Timothy's particular office mentioned, nor his relationship to the church officers that are mentioned.

ii.   *7God doesn't want us to be shy with his gifts, but bold and loving and sensible.* 1Timothy 1 (MSG)

iii.   *15Study to shew thyself approved unto God, a workman that needeth not to be ashamed, rightly dividing the word of truth.* 2Timothy 2 (NKJV)

iv.   *7bInstead, train yourself to be godly. 11Teach these things and insist that everyone learn them.*

v.   *12Don't let anyone think less of you because you are young. Be an example to all believers in what you say, in the way you live, in your love, your faith, and your purity.*

vi.   *13Until I get there, focus on reading the Scriptures to the church, encouraging the believers, and teaching them.*

vii. *¹⁴Do not neglect the spiritual gift you received through the prophecy spoken over you when the elders of the church laid their hands on you.*

Neglect means to overlook, to forget, to be unconcerned, to fail to use.

viii. *¹⁵Give your complete attention to these matters. Throw yourself into your tasks so that everyone will see your progress.* **1Timothy 4 (NLT)**

ix. Submitting ourselves to Mentorship is another sure way to fan, horn and develop our gifts.

Historically, men of God prepared for service through a mentor/mentee relationship with an older preacher. Paul was first mentored by Barnabas. Timothy travelled with Paul, being mentored by the older, more seasoned preacher.

In fact, Paul names multiple individuals he appears to have mentored. In addition to Timothy, among those who accompanied Paul, we know of Titus who served with Paul and was then dispatched to the Isle of Crete.

160

We are also aware of numerous individuals who accompanied Paul at various times during his missionary labours.

Included among these are: Aristarchus (Acts 19;29; Philemon 24; Colossians 4:10), Epaphras (Philemon 23; Colossians 1:7; 4:12), Gaius (Acts 19:29; likely also named in Acts 20:4), Silas (Acts 15:22-40; 16:19-25, 29: 2 Corinthians 1:19), Secundus (ACTS 20:4), Sopater (ACTS 20:4), Trophimus (Acts 20:4; 21:29; 2 Timothy 4:20) and Tychicus (Acts 20:4; Ephesians 6:21).

We also see specifically named as co-workers, fellow prisoners or supporters numerous individuals who may well have been mentored by Paul: Andronicus (ROMANS 16:7), Archippus (Philemon 2; Colossians 4:17), Demas (Philemon 24; Colossians 4:14; see also 2 Timothy 4:10), Epaphroditus (Philippians 2:25; 4:18), Erastus (Acts 19:22; 2 Timothy 4:20), Jason (ACTS 17:5-9), Junia (ROMANS 16:7), Onesiphorus (2 Timothy 1:16; 4:19) and Urbanus (ROMANS 16:9).

There were no Bible schools or seminaries as such, though Paul did interact with disciples on a daily basis in the hall of Tyrannus in Ephesus (see Acts 19:8-10). This appears to be less an instance of formal schooling than a broadly opportunistic implementation of the mentorship Paul had employed.

What is important is to note that Paul appears to have habitually brought gifted individuals into his orbit in order to instruct them, honing the gifts which the Spirit had imparted.

If we follow the model provided in the Word of God, we would encourage all young men who believe themselves called to serve within an eldership to invest time in the presence of older, tested and proven pastors before assuming responsibility for a charge themselves.

Spending time with a seasoned and tested preacher will yield rich benefits for both preachers and congregations.

These gifts are given to the church to build up, encourage, and comfort the church. They are also far more varied than we often realize.

It is easy to think that there are kind of super gifts that people on pedestals have, but if we look at the entirety of the scriptural presentation, there is a remarkable variety of gifts attributed to God's good grace.

1. Prophecy (boldly proclaiming God's mind and purpose) 1 Corinthians 12, 14; Micah 3:8

2. Serving (a wide variety of ministries that "make the dust fly") – 1 Peter 4; 1 Corinthians 12:5

3. Teaching (explaining God's truth) - Romans 12; 1 Corinthians 12; Ephesians 4

    In James 3:1, Christians are cautioned on this gift. The teaching gift will receive a stricter measure of judgement. In other words, teachers will be held more accountable than prophets, evangelists, even apostles etc.

    It is a grave responsibility to become a teacher of the word. Every one of us must account for how he used his gifts but teachers will face a very strict scrutiny because teachers shape the church!

4. Working (bringing energy to a project) - 1 Corinthians 12:6

5. Exhortation (motivational skills; encouragement) – Romans 12

6. Giving (joyful, sacrificial generosity) - Romans 12

7. Mercy (compassion) – Romans 12

8. Intercession (prayer) - Romans 8:26, 27

9. Wisdom (knowledge rightly applied to situations) - James 1:5; Numbers 27

10. Words of Wisdom (giving insightful, practical knowledge) – 1 Corinthians 12

11. Words of Knowledge (giving insight into doctrine/spiritual truth) – 1 Corinthians 12

12. Faith (unwavering commitment and trust that God works beyond human capabilities; good at encouraging others to trust in God in the face of apparently insurmountable odds)– 1 Corinthians 12

13. Healing (miraculous interventions for sickness) - 1 Corinthians 12

14. Miracles – (supernatural acts) - 1 Corinthians 12

15. Discerning spirits (insight into the "spirit" of a situation) – 1 Corinthians 12

16. Tongues (gifted in human or heavenly languages) – 1 Corinthians 12, 14

It is not every Christian that believes all these spiritual gifts are still given by God today. Some think that there were certain gifts, such as speaking in tongues, that were handed down only for a time when they were needed in biblical history and are no longer needed now. I do not wish to dabble into that theological argument here.

Speaking in tongues is one of the spiritual gifts surrounded with many controversies. Speaking in tongues has become the number 1 identity of the Pentecostals but it must be clear, that this gift did not originate from 21st century Pentecostal church pastors, it is a spiritual gift powered by God.

Never is it mentioned in scripture that this gift is withdrawn from the church of God, it still active. Speaking in tongues is the only language that the devil does not understand. It is a coded discussion between the spirit of the speaker and God himself. It edifies the speaker alone.

It is not necessary that the speaker understands what he is saying. If he has the gift of interpretation of tongues, he will understand what he is saying but if he does not have that gift, he will not know what he himself is saying except when someone with the gift interprets. The gift of tongues needs the augment of the gift of interpretation.

17. Interpretation of Tongues – (translating those languages) 1 Corinthians 12, 14

Without speaking in tongues, this gift is of no use because it only interprets speaking in tongues.

18. Apostle (in one sense, unique to the founding of the church; the 'apostolic gift' is probably best understood now as 'church planting') – 1 Corinthians 12; Ephesians 4

Christians disagree on the subject of this gift. Some people claim that some of the gifts were temporary gifts, being of special use during the apostolic era which were later withdrawn, or have become inoperative.

The gift of apostleship is an example of such gifts that some people believed were withdrawn. They claim that "In its technical and narrow sense, there are no more apostles today, since they had to be men who walked and talked with the Lord Jesus, and had seen the risen Christ." Such people appeals to the book of Acts 1:21-25; I Cor. 9:1 as the basis of their claim.

However, I have studied these passages they so claim as their basis and many other passages that concerns the gift of apostleship. My findings from scripture contradict their claim. I believe that the gift of apostleship is not withdrawn.

If Paul who was formerly Saul is regarded in scripture as an apostle, then the claim that apostles must be men who walked and talked with the Lord Jesus, and had seen the risen Christ is not very sound.

Paul did not walk and talk with the Lord Jesus during his earthly days neither had he seen the risen Christ. Paul met the risen Lord on the Damascus road vision. And so, we cannot argue that there are no apostles today.

I personally know so few who claim to be called by God to occupy the office of apostles in our day: Apostles Joshua Nimmak Selman, Micheal Orokpo, Johnson Suleiman, Arome Osayi, etc.

I respect all these men I mentioned; I have no doubt whatsoever about their calling as apostles. None of them was in the earthly days of Jesus Christ but like Paul, they also have testimony that they at different points in times encountered the Lord Jesus who commissioned them for the office.

19. Leadership (church planters and church sustainers) – Romans 12

20. Pastor ("shepherds" who guide and lead) – Ephesians 4

21. Evangelist/Missionary (boldness in sharing the gospel) - Acts 1:8; 5:32; 26:22; 1 John 5:6; Ephesians 4

22. Helps (helping/serving the poor and downtrodden) - 1 Corinthians 12; 1 Timothy 3:8-13; Romans 16:1-4; 12

23. Administration (the ability to give oversight) - 1 Corinthians 12; 1 Samuel 11 and 16

24. Celibacy (refraining from sex with purity) - 1 Corinthians 7:7, Matthew 19:11-12

25. Marriage (committing to a covenant with integrity) - 1 Corinthians 7:7

26. Hospitality (openness and friendliness) - 1 Peter 4:9-10

27. Craftsmanship (building, construction) - Exodus 31:3; 35:30-35

28. The Arts (music, poetry, prose, painting...) – Exodus 31:2-6; Exodus 35:25-26; Psalm 150:3-5 Luke 1:1-3

29. Voluntary Poverty (forgoing wealth without envy, jealousy or judgment of others) - 1 Corinthians 13:1-3

30. Business Sense (reward from hard work and investment) -Ecclesiastes 3,5

31. Courage (as seen in Gideon) - Judges 6

32. Strength (as seen in Samson) - Judges 13

33. Architectural Engineering (planning; constructing; building) - 1 Chronicles 28

Prayer: Dear Gracious Lord, thank You for the unique natural and spiritual gifts You have given me. Holy Spirit please help and teach me to discover, guard, develop and deploy these abilities for the growth and expansion of God's Kingdom on earth, in Jesus' name. Amen.

Discovering the gifts God has given us

Earlier this year when the shepherd in charge of our local assembly was introducing the theme "Occupy till I come", he asked to see how many people in the congregation knew their spiritual gifts. Only about 10 persons lifted up their hands. This is tragic!

Majority of those in attendance said they do not know their spiritual gift, in fact, some said they do not even know their natural ability (talent that they possess).

I have an elder brother (Ayuba Bitrus Galadima) who is so gifted with the spiritual ability to counsel couples whose marriages are going through rough moments. Ayuba was already putting this gift to use without knowing that he was doing what he was doing because he had a gift.

When God helped me to discover that, I approached him concerning it and told him about it and encouraged him to guard the gift, develop the gift and become more deliberate and proactive in using the gift.

Again, I have another elder brother (Silas Jatau Tukura) whom I noticed was gifted with the spiritual enablement of encouraging and motivating people to give and donate their substance for the work of ministry.

Our local assembly identified that potential in him and has since been engaging him whenever there is need to encourage the people of God to give their resources for kingdom advancement. Indeed he is using this gift but I must say that he will need to further fan, horn, and stir and develop this gift for full maximization.

But there are many who possess spiritual gifts without even knowing that they possess the gift. An unopened gift is worthless according Rick Warren. Ignorance of our spiritual gifts is mostly the cause of trouble in the church.

Two common problems are "gift-envy" and "gift-projection." The first (gift-envy) occurs when we compare ourselves with others', feel dissatisfied with what we are, and become resentful or jealous of how God uses others.

The second (gift-projection) problem happens when we expect everyone else to have our kinds of gifts, do what we are called to do, and feel as passionate about it as we do. We can trace so many problems in the church to these two roots. However, these can be avoided if we each will find, discover and know our individual gifts.

There are two approaches to discovering spiritual gifts:

1. The first approach is the intentional investigation by the individual to discover the spiritual gifts he possesses. This is a journey of self-discovery.

2. The second approach is the intentional investigation of the spiritual gifts of someone to help him/her to discover the gifts he possesses. This is not done by the individual himself; but someone else does examine him/her to find out the gifts of God at work in him/her. Usually this person who examines people to discover their spiritual gifts is either their pastor or priest, or the person's spiritual mentor.

1. How to discover your gifts personally

In this section, we shall explore how you shall undertake a journey of discovering your spiritual gift.

i.   Know that you possess at least one spiritual gift. It is expected that you are born again before you begin discussing the possibility of having a spiritual gift because spiritual gifts are only for people who have accepted the Lord Jesus as their personal Lord and Savior.

If you are not born into the natural world you will not have natural talents. Likewise, if you are not born again spiritually, you cannot be given spiritual gifts (Acts 2:38).

ii. Study the scriptures to know the many spiritual gifts that are available for the church. For if you do not know what spiritual gifts exist, you will not be able to recognize the ones that God has given you.

In 2018 and sometimes around 2020, Alex Ibrahim Maikarfi the director of MISTLAND[27] urged me to join translation work but I refused. I never knew what he saw and why he wanted me to join the Translation ministry, so, I refused until March 2022 when I joined MISTLAND.

I was amazed to find that the technical translation gift of creating parallel reference, footnotes, cross references and verse by verse commentaries was something I have been doing on my own since 2013 immediately after I was baptized by the Holy Spirit.

---

[27] MISTLAND is Mission For Scripture Translation and Language Development. It is a Bible Translation organization with its headquarters in Minna Niger State, Nigeria. The organization is committed to developing indigenous Nigerian languages and the training of technical personnel needed for language development. Currently, MISTLAND is working with and developing 5 language projects: Ẹda and Jijili languages (Niger State) and Ẹhua, Ajuele and Ajigha languages (Kaduna State).

I realized that I have been doing that on my study bible for about 8 to 9 years ago and Alex has never seeing any of my study material but he had the spiritual understanding of knowing that I have spiritual gifts needful for Bible Translation.

The reason for my ignorance of this very spiritual gift that I possess was because I never knew that there is a gift as that. I had the ability but I never knew that such ability was a gift.

That is why you must know what spiritual gifts exist and it is my own believe that as you were reading through the descriptions of gifts listed above, some of them resonate with you. Perhaps such gifts that resonate with you could be the gift or gifts you have been given.

iii. You can ask your Christian friends which gifts they identify in you—very often they can see what you cannot and can observe which skills God has divinely assigned to you.

I have been privileged to have these kind of friends. Their list includes Isuwa Samuel Chitumu, Gabriel Daniel Ibrahim, Joseph John amongst others. They readily see the gift divinely assigned to me and they told me. Just last two months, Isuwa told me that I am a replica of Bro. Gbile Akanni. Now that does not mean I am his equal but it does mean that I have a teaching gift that closely resembles his own.

Again, you can observe Models of the Gifts: As you are considering what gifts you might have, it is helpful to observe "mature models[28]" of the various gifts. Talk with them and ask them questions:

How do you know you had the gift of so-so?
How did you begin to use it?
How did you develop the gift?
Are there specific things I must avoid to maximize this gift?

Learning how others discovered their gifts and observing mature models of gifts in action will help you identify your own gift.

iv.   You can pray about it; if we ask God to lead us toward whatever gifts He has given us, he can make it clearer to us.

v.   Some churches offer spiritual gifts classes to help you discover yours. Ask a leader at your church if this is something they offer. The analysis of your spiritual abilities by a Christian leader is indeed very needful if you cannot discover your own spiritual gift from (i) one to (iv).

vi.   You can also take an online spiritual gifts test—simply search online and you will find one. But note that the test may not be reliable, so do not take the results hook line and sinker and be sure to keep pursuing the answer in prayer.

---

[28] A Mature Model of a spiritual gift is a believer who has been effectively using a gift for an extended period of time.

2. How to analyze the spiritual gifts of others to discover the spiritual gifts they possess

This majorly is a practical duty of any one who assumes spiritual leadership over others. It is necessary to know the spiritual gifts of your church members to enable you to deploy them into the ministry they are best fit for.

To do this, both you and your followers must have knowledge of spiritual gifts. Then you must prayerfully guide the concerned members of your church through the following steps of discovering spiritual gifts:

1. Check to see if the person is born again. If they are not born again, then, suffer not to go further because God cannot give spiritual gifts to a person who is not saved.

   If he/she is saved, then you can continue the process. However, you may also wish to lead the person to Christ to qualify him to receive spiritual gifts.

2. You may want to verify if the person has received baptism of the Holy Spirit.

3. Give members a detailed knowledge of the various spiritual gifts that are available.

4. Pray and ask God to reveal their gifts.

5. Ask each member to take self-analysis of his spiritual interest.

6. Conduct an analysis of the spiritual gifts of your members as their spiritual leader.

7. Ask each member to take a self-analysis of his past Christian service.

8. Identify the spiritual gifts they might have.
9. Provide a "List of Ministry Needs" to your church members. I shall include a list of Ministry Needs adopted from the work of Bauta Motty.

10. Help them to match their spiritual gift to a ministry need.

11. Conduct a follow up evaluation of their ministry in this area.

Please remember that you must follow these analysis steps prayerfully to analyze the spiritual gifts of your members. Once this is completed and God graciously helps you to discover the gifts of your members, make a chart showing the names of members and the spiritual gifts that God has revealed to you.

A List of Ministry Needs

Below is a list of ministry needs adopted from the book "Mobilization in Leadership" written by Bauta Motty, where any emphasis is added, it is enclosed in a bracket;

i) Visitation: This is a team of members who visit sick persons, newcomers to church, hospitals, widows, prisons, the bereaved, orphanage, home for aged. Individuals concerned with this ministry will need the gifts of healing and comfort to function effectively.

ii) Evangelism: House-to-house, evangelistic services, crusades, open air services.

iii) Follow up Ministry: To new converts.

iv) Office/administrative Support: Typing, drawing, filling, assembling, reproducing materials, mailings, telephones, records.

v) Hospitality: Cooking meals and providing lodging for those in need or for visiting minsters, evangelists, Christians.

vi) Ministry to the Poor: Providing food, clothing, and shelter.

vii) Maintenance or Church Building: Buildings, Landscaping, painting, carpentry, electrical, plumbing, cleaning.

viii) Music: Choir, instruments, song leader, special music groups, soloist, writing music (people like Stephen Maisamari who are gifted to write choir songs will fit into this ministry niche if they pay the price to develop their gift).

ix) Religious drama productions.

x) Financial: Fund raising, accounting, financial planning for ministries.

xi) Writing: Christian books, newsletters, tracts, news and magazine articles, poetry.

xii) Multi-media: Audio and video tapes, radio, television, satellite broadcasting.

xiii) Counseling: General counseling or to specific groups; telephone counseling.

xiv) Ministry to Special Groups: deaf, blind, mentally ill, narcotic addicts, alcoholics, migrant workers, IDPs, gangs, unwed mothers, homosexuals, Jews, minority groups, women, men, families, married couples, abused children, runaways, school dropouts, illiterate, prisoners, military, children, youth, aged.

xv) Church Offices: Elder, deacon/deaconess, Sunday school teacher, usher, committees such as building, finance, etc.

xvi)   Translation: Bible and Christian literature.

xvii)   Christian Education: Sunday School, Vacation Bible school, Christian preschool, elementary high school, college; training for laymen and home Bible studies.

xviii) Missionary/Church Planting: To unreached peoples in your region/nation.

xix)   Literature: Christian library, bookstore, Bible and Christian literature distribution.

The journey of helping your followers to discover their spiritual gifts is rigorous but it all worth it. It must be done to enable you and your followers accomplish the spiritual purposes and objectives for which believers are called. Ephesians 4:12-15.

If you do not know your spiritual gifts, you will want to copy what Mr. A is doing when in spiritual reality, God did not craft you for that specific assignment.

Knowing your spiritual gift will help you to avoid frustration which usually comes from trying to fulfill a spiritual function with natural strength. You will notice that a person who is specially gifted for that work will do so with ease but you will sweat it out and still be unable to do effectively.

Discovering your spiritual gift will help you to fulfill your personal destiny in the body of Christ.

For further reading:
Read "Mobilisation In Leadership" By Bauta Motty. The book is a classic on mobilization against the prevailing manipulative trends in the church.

Read "Learning To Lead: Biblical Leadership, Then and Now" By Chua Wee Hian.

Read "The Purpose Driven Life" By Rick Warren. After the Bible, the book is the best guide for purpose discovery, development, and maximization. It is the instructional manual for purposeful living.

What To Do Wth Your Spiritual Gifts

Learning about spiritual gifts and trying to discover your own gifts is a fun subject because you will get to discover something about yourself that you may not have known before.

Once you determine which gift or gifts you have, start using them to glorify God. By using your spiritual gifts to volunteer in a ministry or around your church, you are moving the Kingdom of God forward. And that applies no matter how small the job may seem.

Find a place to serve (sometimes volunteering is referred to as "serving") that utilizes at least one of your gifts, and you will be amazed at how blessed your time will be. You may notice how easy you find it; God has given you a divine gift that you are inherently good at, and a talent that just comes naturally! You may be surprised at how much you enjoy flexing that new gift muscle too.

The best place to start is at your church; ask a leader where volunteers are needed and see what might fit for your gifting. For example, if you have the gift of mercy, a hospital or prison ministry may be the right place for you. Or if you have the gift of hospitality, greeting new people or setting up for events may be the best fit. The gift of exhortation could make you an amazing addition to a prayer ministry.

Remember that your gifts can be used in many different ways, so do not feel like you have to do something just because it looks, on the surface, as if it is perfect for your gifts. If an assignment is not filling you with joy, find an opportunity that does. Joy is a great indicator of what your gift may be; if a task makes you happy, that is a good sign you have found your skill and fit.

Now go and discover what gifts God has given you, and make sure to use those gifts in the Kingdom!

AN EXTRA WORD!

Occupy Till I Come

Ninety percent (90%) of Nigerian Christians were plagued with a very wrong theology, an evil mindset that made Christians think that some certain offices and jobs are disgusting and sinful to the Christian life.

An example of such is politics. For many decades, Christians have been calling politics a dirty game. They so claim that a person who desires to remain faithful in serving the Lord will not dabble into politics.

For that reason, Christians relaxed their political muscles and ignored their duty to occupy. They left this very influential facet of life to Muslims.

But the master wants us even political offices for him. If we allow all these offices for the enemies of our master, they will occupy them and enforce laws and regulations that will disfavor us.

We must stop the erroneous claim that we are not of the world to mean that occupying earthly positions for the Lord is sinful. No position and no earthly space is too small and no earthly space must be despised, the master is interested in them all.

- It is my belief that the master wants us to occupy some shops in the major markets before he return.

- The master wants us to occupy political, financial and academic positions before he returns.

- The master wants us to occupy some strategic standpoints in the medical field before he return.

- The master wants us to occupy the military before he return.
- The master wants us to occupy the tertiary institutions before he return.

- The master wants us to occupy the teaching profession before he return.

- The master wants us to occupy teaching profession before he return.

The Four Mindset that Crippled Christianity in Nigeria

1. Bringing someone to replace you. Make sure you groom someone to be next to you in your office. It is folly to vacate or retire out of an office with no possibility of a Christian successor. The non-Christians are strictly following this principle to weaken the grip of Christianity in our nations.

   Please get a copy of my book, "The Lepers: heralds of economic revival" for more on this point. I discussed this in a section titled a word for Adunu.

2. Avoiding politics because we are thinking politics is a dirty game

3. No deliberate strategic plan for the years to come

4. We are only reactive and not proactive. We do not strike but only wait to retaliate. In Money heist, a film I watched, I learnt from the professor who was the leader of the gang how to place yourself on the advantage by striking or attacking first.

    The person who takes the time to plan ahead, will predict the possible reaction of his opponent and how to counter him. While the opponent is still entrapped in shock, and only acting reactively, with no time to figure out exactly what will happen next, the person who strike first will forge ahead with the step of his plan while his opponent and still trying to defend the first.

5. Separating religion from our daily life. Christians do not carry their religion to their offices. They do not see themselves as servants of the master who are occupying the office for the master.

    Christians must learn to make their offices and every position they hold as an outpost for the Lord. What I mean by that is that, you must learn to think of how to prioritize Christianity over any other religion in the very office you are holding.

If there are 5 positions to be given and you have 5 Christians and 5 non-Christians applying for the positions, then give 3 or 4 seats to the Christian and 1 or 2 seats to the non-Christian.

Do not be afraid of the insult and their complaint. Remember, that is what they do and even if you complain the whole day, nothing change. Because, for them, religion cannot be separated from their day to day living, their religion is first.

You must never join hands to support any protest to remove a Christian who is occupying any position except if it is another Christian that will still occupy it. Do not support anybody to remove a Christian from a position that you know that it is a non-Christians that will replace him.

If you agree to join a protest to remove your brother, you will be a fool because the non-Christians can never join hands with you to impeach their brother whatever be the case. Learn a lesson from this slogan, "***Monkey no fine but him mama like am***

HOPE

[7]"At least there is hope for a tree: If it is cut down, it will sprout again, and its new shoots will not fail. [8]Its roots may grow old in the ground and its stump die in the soil, [9]yet at the scent of water it will bud and put forth shoots like a plant.

Job 14 (NIV)

Hope is a confident desire: a strong feeling that something desirable is likely to happen even when the prevailing situation is contrary and unlikely. Hope is that which gives an individual the feeling of likelihood of success: a chance that something desirable will happen or be possible.

It is a confident belief that things will improve even when they are bad. Hope is positivity in negativity! Hope is the spirit that heals all diseases, redeems lives from destruction, and brings sunshine back after the rain: people who have it endure through the storms. They try even when they fail and dare to rise again even when it seems hopeless.

It is hope that makes the righteous to rise seven times after falling seven times. That is what you need. You may have failed to use your God-given abilities. You may have wasted the investment of God in your life. Yet, I have a word for you, there is hope!

No matter how old you think you are, there is still hope. You can still embark on a journey of discovering your God-given talents and abilities and use them even now that you are old. Fear may have forced you to bury your own minas because you afraid of trying or afraid of what people would say. God's word to you is this – at least, there is hope!

You may have gone too long in your job with only one stream of income. You may be retiring next year with just a stream of income and you fear how life after retirement would be. Having gone through my counsel on multiple streams of income, you must not give up hope but let hope rise in your heart.

You can begin something today. It is possible you are not used to trading and business and shame of starting is not allowing you to start. There is still hope if you will just give it a leap of faith.

Failure to embrace hope is willingly embracing hopelessness. Hopelessness breeds only one thing, impossibility! It is the building block of misery. It wanes passion and enthusiasm. No matter you may have failed, please try!

www.ingramcontent.com/pod-product-compliance
Lightning Source LLC
Chambersburg PA
CBHW070543220526
45467CB00003B/1035